Mini Cupcakes

by
Leslie Fiet

photographs by
Zac Williams

GIBBS SMITH
TO ENRICH AND INSPIRE HUMANKIND

First Edition
15 14 13 12 11   5 4 3

Text © 2011 Leslie Fiet
Photographs © 2011 Zac Williams

All rights reserved. No part of this book may be reproduced by any means whatsoever without written permission from the publisher, except brief portions quoted for purpose of review.

Published by
Gibbs Smith
P.O. Box 667
Layton, Utah 84041

1.800.835.4993 orders
www.gibbs-smith.com

www.mini-cupcakes.com

Designed by Sugar Design
Printed and bound in China
Gibbs Smith books are printed on either recycled, 100% post-consumer waste, FSC-certified papers or on paper produced from sustainable PEFC-certified forest/controlled wood source. Learn more at www.pefc.org.

Library of Congress Cataloging-in-Publication Data

Fiet, Leslie.
  Mini cupcakes / Leslie Fiet ; photographs by Zac Williams. — 1st ed.
      p. cm.
  Includes index.
  ISBN 978-1-4236-1808-9
  1. Cupcakes. I. Title.
  TX771.F54 2011
  641.8'653—dc22
                                2010038389

CONTENTS

Introduction	4
Buttery Vanilla	6
Chocolate	20
Fruit & Citrus	58
Coffee & Libations	74
Index	93

introduction

MINI BAKING BASICS

All the recipes in this cookbook have been created using a convection oven and a KitchenAid mixer. If you are using a regular baking oven without convection setting, your baking times may be longer by as much as 5 to 10 minutes. If you use a hand mixer, watch for the look of the cupcake and frosting as it is described in the recipe. The mixing times may be longer to achieve the same results.

TOOLS OF THE TRADE AND BASIC INGREDIENTS

The following are items you should have on hand when you bake and decorate your cupcakes to ensure you will have a fun and enjoyable experience. If you have all of these pantry items, you can make any combination of any cupcake, frosting, or filling in this book. All recipes call for soybean oil, but you can substitute vegetable or canola oil. Many recipes call for buttermilk; there are tips for making your own buttermilk with lemon juice and milk, if necessary.

Most of these ingredients may be purchased through your local grocer; however, some items, such as vanilla bean paste, are more commonly available at specialty food markets.

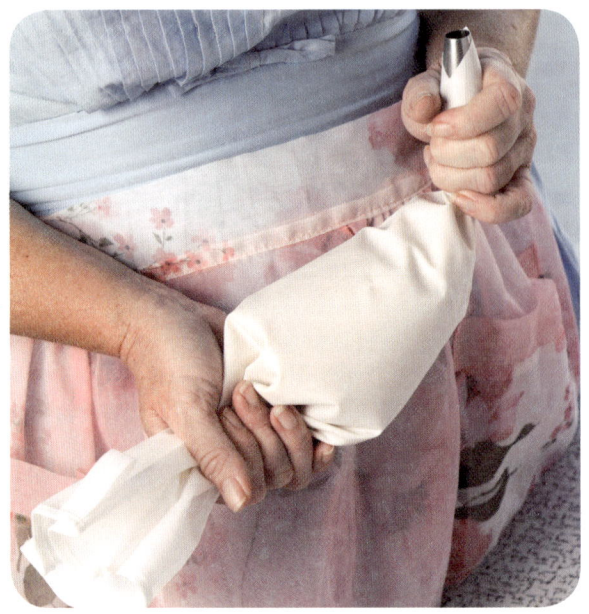

Baking Tools
2-ounce paper soufflé cups
    (commonly called nut cups)
Flat baking sheets
Silpat or parchment paper
18-inch pastry bag (two or more)
Round #806 pastry tip (two or more)
Apple corer
Large zester

In the Pantry
Unbleached flour
Granulated sugar
Powdered sugar
Espresso powder
Light corn syrup
Guittard extra-dark chocolate
    chips, at least 62% cacao
Guittard white chocolate chips
Dutch-process cocoa powder
Soybean oil (may substitute
    vegetable or canola oil)
Unsweetened applesauce
Vanilla
Vanilla bean paste
Baking powder
Salt
Pecans
Canned beets
Champagne vinegar

Margarita mix (dry)
Assorted colors of sanding sugars,
    silver dragées, nonpareils
Assorted colors of coloring gel paste

In the Fridge
Fresh eggs
Unsalted butter
Cream cheese
Sour cream
Milk
Heavy cream
Buttermilk
Fresh lemons and key limes
Fresh and frozen berries
Lemon juice
Key lime juice
Bananas, ripe or frozen

BUTTERY VANILLA

Pretty in Pink
9

The Audrey
11

Tainted Love
14

Snowball
17

Pretty in Pink

Mini's Buttery Vanilla Cupcakes
Mini's Cream Cheese Frosting, tinted light pink
Pink and white sanding sugar for decoration

Makes 30 cupcakes in perfectly cute 2-ounce soufflé cups

wet ingredients

- ¼ cup sour cream
- ¼ cup buttermilk
- ½ cup unsweetened applesauce
- ½ cup soybean oil
- ¼ cup unsalted butter, room temperature
- 2 large eggs
- 1 egg yolk
- 2 tablespoons vanilla
- 1 tablespoon vanilla bean paste

dry ingredients

- 2 cups unbleached flour
- 1 cup sugar
- 1¼ tablespoons baking powder
- ½ teaspoon salt

MINI'S BUTTERY VANILLA CUPCAKES

BEFORE YOU START: *Preheat oven to 350 degrees F.*

Place 30 soufflé cups on a flat baking sheet lined with parchment paper or a Silpat.

Place an 18-inch pastry bag with tip inside a large cup with the outside edge hanging over. You will use this to fill the soufflé cups with cupcake batter.

1. Place all wet ingredients together in a mixing bowl. Mix on low speed with a wire whisk attachment for about 1 minute until all ingredients are blended.

2. Combine all dry ingredients in a separate bowl and stir with a spoon to combine.

3. Add dry ingredients to wet ingredients and blend on low for 1 minute until combined. Batter will be lumpy but blended. Scrape down the sides of the bowl. Turn mixer on high for 30 seconds; most of the lumps will disappear and small air bubbles will start to form.

4. Pour batter into prepared pastry bag, then carefully pick up bag and hold the tip upright to prevent the batter from spilling out. Fill the soufflé cups half full.

5. Bake for 17 minutes. Cupcakes are done when you can apply light pressure to the top of the cupcake and it bounces back.

Pretty in Pink
continued

- 1 (8-ounce) package cream cheese, room temperature
- 1 tablespoon vanilla
- 4 cups powdered sugar
- Food coloring (optional)

MINI'S CREAM CHEESE FROSTING

Frosts 25 to 30 cupcakes

1. In a mixing bowl with a wire whisk attachment, beat the cream cheese and vanilla for 3 to 4 minutes. Continually scrape down sides of bowl to ensure all the cream cheese is creamy and well blended.

2. Slowly add the powdered sugar, about $1/2$ cup at a time, to the mixture. If you are going to tint the frosting, add the food coloring about halfway through the powdered sugar addition. Mix in each addition of powdered sugar completely, as this will eliminate lumps. Scrape down the bowl often.

Assembly

After cupcakes have cooled, use your piping bag to frost each cupcake and top with pink and white sanding sugar.

The Audrey

Mini's Buttery Vanilla Cupcakes
Mini's Cream Cheese Frosting, tinted light blue
Silver dragées, white nonpareils, and white sugar pearls for decoration

Makes 30 cupcakes in perfectly cute 2-ounce soufflé cups

wet ingredients

- ¼ cup sour cream
- ¼ cup buttermilk
- ½ cup unsweetened applesauce
- ½ cup soybean oil
- ¼ cup unsalted butter, room temperature
- 2 large eggs
- 1 egg yolk
- 2 tablespoons vanilla
- 1 tablespoon vanilla bean paste

dry ingredients

- 2 cups unbleached flour
- 1 cup sugar
- 1¼ tablespoons baking powder
- ½ teaspoon salt

MINI'S BUTTERY VANILLA CUPCAKES

BEFORE YOU START: *Preheat oven to 350 degrees F.*

Place 30 soufflé cups on a flat baking sheet lined with parchment paper or a Silpat.

Place an 18-inch pastry bag with tip inside a large cup with the outside edge hanging over. You will use this to fill the soufflé cups with cupcake batter.

1. Place all wet ingredients together in a mixing bowl. Mix on low speed with a wire whisk attachment for about 1 minute until all ingredients are blended.

2. Combine all dry ingredients in a separate bowl and stir with a spoon to combine.

3. Add dry ingredients to wet ingredients and blend on low for 1 minute until combined. Batter will be lumpy but blended. Scrape down the sides of the bowl. Turn mixer on high for 30 seconds; most of the lumps will disappear and small air bubbles will start to form.

4. Pour batter into prepared pastry bag, then carefully pick up bag and hold the tip upright to prevent the batter from spilling out. Fill the soufflé cups half full.

The Audrey
continued

1 (8-ounce) package cream cheese, room temperature
1 tablespoon vanilla
4 cups powdered sugar
Food coloring (optional)

5. Bake for 17 minutes. Cupcakes are done when you can apply light pressure to the top of the cupcake and it bounces back.

MINI'S CREAM CHEESE FROSTING

Frosts 25 to 30 cupcakes

1. In a mixing bowl with a wire whisk attachment, beat the cream cheese and vanilla for 3 to 4 minutes. Continually scrape down sides of bowl to ensure all the cream cheese is creamy and well blended.

2. Slowly add the powdered sugar, about $1/2$ cup at a time, to the mixture. If you are going to tint the frosting, add the food coloring about halfway through the powdered sugar addition. Mix in each addition of powdered sugar completely, as this will eliminate lumps. Scrape down the bowl often.

Assembly

After your cupcakes have cooled, use your piping bag to frost each cupcake and top with silver dragées, white nonpareils, and white sugar pearls.

Tainted Love

Mini's Buttery Vanilla Cupcakes
Dark Chocolate Ganache Frosting
Pink and white nonpareils for decoration

Makes 30 cupcakes in perfectly cute 2-ounce soufflé cups

wet ingredients

- ¼ cup sour cream
- ¼ cup buttermilk
- ½ cup unsweetened applesauce
- ½ cup soybean oil
- ¼ cup unsalted butter, room temperature
- 2 large eggs
- 1 egg yolk
- 2 tablespoons vanilla
- 1 tablespoon vanilla bean paste

dry ingredients

- 2 cups unbleached flour
- 1 cup sugar
- 1¼ tablespoons baking powder
- ½ teaspoon salt

MINI'S BUTTERY VANILLA CUPCAKES

BEFORE YOU START: *Preheat oven to 350 degrees F.*

Place 30 soufflé cups on a flat baking sheet lined with parchment paper or a Silpat.

Place an 18-inch pastry bag with tip inside a large cup with the outside edge hanging over. You will use this to fill the soufflé cups with cupcake batter.

1. Place all wet ingredients together in a mixing bowl. Mix on low speed with a wire whisk attachment for about 1 minute until all ingredients are blended.

2. Combine all dry ingredients in a separate bowl and stir with a spoon to combine.

3. Add dry ingredients to wet ingredients and blend on low for 1 minute until combined. Batter will be lumpy but blended. Scrape down the sides of the bowl. Turn mixer on high for 30 seconds; most of the lumps will disappear and small air bubbles will start to form.

4. Pour batter into prepared pastry bag, then carefully pick up bag and hold the tip upright to prevent the batter from spilling out. Fill the soufflé cups half full.

5. Bake for 17 minutes. Cupcakes are done when you can apply light pressure to the top of the cupcake and it bounces back.

- 2 cups heavy whipping cream
- 2 cups Guittard Extra-Dark Chocolate Chips (62 percent cacao)

DARK CHOCOLATE GANACHE FROSTING

Frosts 25 to 30 cupcakes

NOTE: *Make this frosting the day before you plan on using it, then whip it right before you need it. It really does need to sit overnight and there is no way to rush it.*

1. Pour the cream in a mixing bowl, and place the bowl over a pan of simmering water. Heat the cream until it starts to boil and climb the sides of the bowl. Watch it closely: when the cream starts to rise it can very easily boil over.

2. Carefully remove the mixing bowl from the boiling water. Add the chocolate chips to the cream and let rest for about 5 minutes. Using a whisk, blend the cream and chocolate until the chocolate is fully incorporated. There should be no bits of chocolate left on the whisk.

3. Cover and refrigerate overnight or longer, up to one week.

4. When ready to use, place the mixing bowl back onto your mixer and use the flat paddle attachment to beat the chocolate. Start on low and gradually increase the speed until you see a ridge start to form around the paddle and the chocolate gets stiff. Scrape down the sides of the bowl often. Make sure you do not overbeat the chocolate. If you beat it past seeing ridges and stiffness, it will become grainy.

Assembly

After your cupcakes have cooled, frost each cupcake with Dark Chocolate Ganache Frosting and top with pink and white nonpareils.

Snowball

Mini's Buttery Vanilla Cupcakes
Matterhorn Buttercream Frosting
Shredded coconut
White chocolate for decoration

Makes 30 cupcakes in perfectly cute 2-ounce soufflé cups

wet ingredients

- ¼ cup sour cream
- ¼ cup buttermilk
- ½ cup unsweetened applesauce
- ½ cup soybean oil
- ¼ cup unsalted butter, room temperature
- 2 large eggs
- 1 egg yolk
- 2 tablespoons vanilla
- 1 tablespoon vanilla bean paste

dry ingredients

- 2 cups unbleached flour
- 1 cup sugar
- 1¼ tablespoons baking powder
- ½ teaspoon salt

MINI'S BUTTERY VANILLA CUPCAKES

BEFORE YOU START: *Preheat oven to 350 degrees F.*

Place 30 soufflé cups on a flat baking sheet lined with parchment paper or a Silpat.

Place an 18-inch pastry bag with tip inside a large cup with the outside edge hanging over. You will use this to fill the soufflé cups with cupcake batter.

1. Place all wet ingredients together in a mixing bowl. Mix on low speed with a wire whisk attachment for about 1 minute until all ingredients are blended.

2. Combine all dry ingredients in a separate bowl and stir with a spoon to combine.

3. Add dry ingredients to wet ingredients and blend on low for 1 minute until combined. Batter will be lumpy but blended. Scrape down the sides of the bowl. Turn mixer on high for 30 seconds; most of the lumps will disappear and small air bubbles will start to form.

4. Pour batter into prepared pastry bag, then carefully pick up bag and hold the tip upright to prevent the batter from spilling out. Fill the soufflé cups half full.

5. Bake for 17 minutes. Cupcakes are done when you can apply light pressure to the top of the cupcake and it bounces back.

Snowball continued

- 5 egg whites, room temperature
- 1⅛ cups granulated sugar
- Pinch salt
- 1 teaspoon vanilla
- 2 cups unsalted butter, room temperature
- 2 cups powdered sugar

MATTERHORN BUTTERCREAM FROSTING

Frosts 25 to 30 cupcakes

1. In a mixing bowl, whisk egg whites, sugar, and salt. Place the mixing bowl over a pan of simmering water. Whisk the mixture every couple of minutes to ensure the sugar granules along the side of the bowl are fully melted with the egg. Continue to whisk until temperature reaches 174 degrees F.

2. Remove bowl from the pan of simmering water and beat the mixture on high using a wire whisk attachment until the bottom of the bowl no longer retains any heat and the mixture reaches a stiff peak consistency. Add vanilla; whisk until incorporated.

3. Remove the wire whisk and use the paddle attachment to finish the frosting. With the mixer set on medium-low, add the butter, 1 tablespoon at a time, waiting until each addition of butter is blended in before adding the next. If the frosting becomes curdled, do not worry; just continue to add the butter and beat the frosting, and it will eventually become creamy and smooth.

4. Once all the butter is incorporated and the mixture is creamy and smooth, add the powdered sugar, ½ cup at a time. Continue until all sugar is incorporated. Frosting will be slightly stiff.

1 cup white chocolate or white chocolate bark pieces

DECORATIVE CHOCOLATE DISCS

Makes about 12 discs

1. Melt chocolate in a glass bowl in the microwave or in a metal bowl over a pan of simmering water, stirring frequently. When chocolate is melted and smooth, use a teaspoon and pour a small amount on a chilled flat baking sheet lined with parchment paper. Repeat with remaining melted chocolate. Place in refrigerator and chill. Use discs to decorate the top of cupcakes.

Assembly

After cupcakes have cooled, frost each one with Matterhorn Buttercream Frosting and roll each frosted cupcake in shredded coconut and decorate with a chocolate disc.

The Diva
23

Black and White
27

The Chocoholic
31

Twisted Sister
35

Cookie Monster
39

Mini's Sweet and Salty
43

"CHIP's" The Ponch and Jon
47

PB Fix
49

S'Mores Please
53

Southern Comfort
56

The Diva

Mini's Chocoholic Cupcakes
Mini's Cream Cheese Frosting, tinted light pink
Chocolate discs for decoration

Makes 30 cupcakes in perfectly cute 2-ounce soufflé cups

chocolate ingredients

- ½ cup Guittard Extra-Dark Chocolate Chips, at least 62 percent cacao
- ½ cup boiling water, strong coffee, or espresso

wet ingredients

- ½ cup unsweetened applesauce
- ½ cup soybean oil
- 2 large eggs
- 1 tablespoon vanilla

dry ingredients

- 1½ cups unbleached flour
- 1 cup sugar
- 1 tablespoon baking powder
- ½ teaspoon salt
- ½ cup Dutch-process cocoa powder

MINI'S CHOCOHOLIC CUPCAKES

BEFORE YOU START: *Preheat oven to 350 degrees F.*

Place 30 soufflé cups on a flat baking sheet lined with parchment paper or a Silpat.

Place an 18-inch pastry bag with tip inside a large cup with the outside edge hanging over. You will use this to fill the soufflé cups with cupcake batter.

1. In a large glass measuring cup, combine the chocolate and boiling water. Let the chocolate melt in the hot liquid, then stir to combine and set aside.

2. Place all wet ingredients together in a mixing bowl. Mix on low speed with a wire whisk attachment for about 1 minute until all ingredients are blended. Slowly pour the warm chocolate mixture down the side of the bowl while the mixer is on low. Do not add the hot water and chocolate too quickly or you will cook the eggs.

3. Combine all dry ingredients in a separate bowl and stir with a spoon to combine.

4. Add dry ingredients to wet ingredients and blend on low speed for 30 seconds until combined. Batter will be lumpy. Scrape down the bowl and turn your mixer on high for 30 seconds. Scrape down bowl again and return to high for another 30 seconds.

The Diva continued

5. Pour batter into prepared pastry bag, then carefully pick up bag and hold the tip upright to prevent the batter from spilling out. Fill the soufflé cups half full.

6. Bake cupcakes for 19 minutes. They are done when you can apply light pressure to the top of the cupcake and it bounces back. Also watch for a shiny part in the center of the cupcakes; if there is shine, they have not cooked long enough.

PRO TIP: *It is important to use Dutch-process cocoa in this recipe. The normal grocery store variety of cocoa is usually unsweetened but it has not been treated with an alkali to neutralize its natural acidity.*

---

1 (8-ounce) package cream cheese, room temperature
1 tablespoon vanilla
4 cups powdered sugar
Food coloring (optional)

MINI'S CREAM CHEESE FROSTING

Frosts 25 to 30 cupcakes

1. In a mixing bowl with a wire whisk attachment, beat the cream cheese and vanilla for 3 to 4 minutes. Continually scrape down sides of bowl to ensure all the cream cheese is creamy and well blended.

2. Slowly add the powdered sugar, about ½ cup at a time, to the mixture. If you are going to tint the frosting, add the food coloring about halfway through the powdered sugar addition. Mix in each addition of powdered sugar completely, as this will eliminate lumps. Scrape down the bowl often.

1 cup dark chocolate or chocolate bark pieces
½ cup white chocolate or white chocolate bark pieces
Pink food coloring

DECORATIVE CHOCOLATE DISCS

Makes about 12 discs

1. Melt dark chocolate in a glass bowl in the microwave or in a metal bowl over a pan of simmering water, stirring frequently. When chocolate is melted and smooth, use a teaspoon and pour a small amount on a chilled flat baking sheet lined with parchment paper. Repeat with remaining melted chocolate. Place in refrigerator and chill.

2. Melt white chocolate in a glass bowl in the microwave or in a metal bowl over a pan of simmering water, stirring frequently. When chocolate is melted and smooth, tint with pink dye, then use a fork to drizzle pink chocolate on top of chilled dark chocolate discs. Place in refrigerator and chill.

3. Use discs to decorate the top of cupcakes.

Assembly

After the cupcakes have cooled, use your pastry bag to frost each cupcake; top with chocolate discs.

Black and White

Mini's Chocoholic Cupcakes
Matterhorn Buttercream Frosting
Chocolate discs for decoration

Makes 30 cupcakes in perfectly cute 2-ounce soufflé cups

chocolate ingredients

- ½ cup Guittard Extra-Dark Chocolate Chips, at least 62 percent cacao
- ½ cup boiling water, strong coffee, or espresso

wet ingredients

- ½ cup unsweetened applesauce
- ½ cup soybean oil
- 2 large eggs
- 1 tablespoon vanilla

dry ingredients

- 1½ cups unbleached flour
- 1 cup sugar
- 1 tablespoon baking powder
- ½ teaspoon salt
- ½ cup Dutch-process cocoa powder

MINI'S CHOCOHOLIC CUPCAKES

BEFORE YOU START: *Preheat oven to 350 degrees F.*

Place 30 soufflé cups on a flat baking sheet lined with parchment paper or a Silpat.

Place an 18-inch pastry bag with tip inside a large cup with the outside edge hanging over. You will use this to fill the soufflé cups with cupcake batter.

1. In a large glass measuring cup, combine the chocolate and boiling water. Let the chocolate melt in the hot liquid, then stir to combine and set aside.

2. Place all wet ingredients together in a mixing bowl. Mix on low speed with a wire whisk attachment for about 1 minute until all ingredients are blended. Slowly pour the warm chocolate mixture down the side of the bowl while the mixer is on low. Do not add the hot water and chocolate too quickly or you will cook the eggs.

3. Combine all dry ingredients in a separate bowl and stir with a spoon to combine.

4. Add dry ingredients to wet ingredients and blend on low speed for 30 seconds until combined. Batter will be lumpy. Scrape down the bowl and turn your mixer on high for 30 seconds. Scrape down bowl again, and return to high for another 30 seconds.

Black and White continued

5. Pour batter into prepared pastry bag, then carefully pick up bag and hold the tip upright to prevent the batter from spilling out. Fill the soufflé cups half full.

6. Bake cupcakes for 19 minutes. They are done when you can apply light pressure to the top of the cupcake and it bounces back. Also watch for a shiny part in the center of the cupcakes; if there is shine, they have not cooked long enough.

PRO TIP: *It is important to use Dutch-process cocoa in this recipe. The normal grocery store variety of cocoa is usually unsweetened but it has not been treated with an alkali to neutralize its natural acidity.*

---

5 egg whites, room temperature
1⅛ cups granulated sugar
Pinch salt
1 teaspoon vanilla
2 cups unsalted butter, room temperature
2 cups powdered sugar

MATTERHORN BUTTERCREAM FROSTING

Frosts 25 to 30 cupcakes

1. In a mixing bowl, whisk egg whites, sugar, and salt. Place the mixing bowl over a pan of simmering water. Whisk the mixture every couple of minutes to ensure the sugar granules along the side of the bowl are fully melted with the egg. Continue to whisk until temperature reaches 174 degrees F.

2. Remove bowl from the pan of simmering water and beat the mixture on high using a wire whisk attachment until the bottom of the bowl no longer retains any heat and the mixture reaches a stiff peak consistency. Add vanilla; whisk until incorporated.

3. Remove the wire whisk and use the paddle attachment to finish the frosting. With the mixer set on medium-low,

add the butter, 1 tablespoon at a time, waiting until each addition of butter is blended in before adding the next. If the frosting becomes curdled, do not worry; just continue to add the butter and beat the frosting, and it will eventually become creamy and smooth.

4. Once all the butter is incorporated and the mixture is creamy and smooth, add the powdered sugar, 1/2 cup at a time. Continue until all sugar is incorporated. Frosting will be slightly stiff.

---

1 cup dark chocolate or chocolate bark pieces

1/2 cup white chocolate or white chocolate bark pieces

DECORATIVE CHOCOLATE DISCS

Makes about 12 discs

1. Melt dark chocolate in a glass bowl in the microwave or in a metal bowl over a pan of simmering water, stirring frequently. When chocolate is melted and smooth, use a teaspoon and pour a small amount on a chilled flat baking sheet lined with parchment paper. Repeat with remaining melted chocolate. Place in refrigerator and chill.

2. Melt white chocolate in a glass bowl in the microwave or in a metal bowl over a pan of simmering water, stirring frequently. When chocolate is melted and smooth, use the top end of a wooden spoon to place a dot of white chocolate on top of chilled dark chocolate discs. Place in refrigerator and chill.

3. Use discs to decorate the top of cupcakes.

Assembly

After the cupcakes have cooled, use your pastry bag to frost each cupcake; top with chocolate discs.

The Chocoholic

Mini's Chocoholic Cupcakes
Dark Chocolate Ganache Frosting
Chocolate discs and chocolate drizzle for decorations

Makes 30 cupcakes in perfectly cute 2-ounce soufflé cups

chocolate ingredients

- ½ cup Guittard Extra-Dark Chocolate Chips, at least 62 percent cacao
- ½ cup boiling water, strong coffee, or espresso

wet ingredients

- ½ cup unsweetened applesauce
- ½ cup soybean oil
- 2 large eggs
- 1 tablespoon vanilla

dry ingredients

- 1½ cups unbleached flour
- 1 cup sugar
- 1 tablespoon baking powder
- ½ teaspoon salt
- ½ cup Dutch-process cocoa powder

MINI'S CHOCOHOLIC CUPCAKES

BEFORE YOU START: *Preheat oven to 350 degrees F.*

Place 30 soufflé cups on a flat baking sheet lined with parchment paper or a Silpat.

Place an 18-inch pastry bag with tip inside a large cup with the outside edge hanging over. You will use this to fill the soufflé cups with cupcake batter.

1. In a large glass measuring cup, combine the chocolate and boiling water. Let the chocolate melt in the hot liquid, then stir to combine and set aside.

2. Place all wet ingredients together in a mixing bowl. Mix on low speed with a wire whisk attachment for about 1 minute until all ingredients are blended. Slowly pour the warm chocolate mixture down the side of the bowl while the mixer is on low. Do not add the hot water and chocolate too quickly or you will cook the eggs.

3. Combine all dry ingredients in a separate bowl and stir with a spoon to combine.

4. Add dry ingredients to wet ingredients and blend on low speed for 30 seconds until combined. Batter will be lumpy. Scrape down the bowl and turn your mixer on high for 30 seconds. Scrape down bowl again, and return to high for another 30 seconds.

The Chocoholic continued

5. Pour batter into prepared pastry bag, then carefully pick up bag and hold the tip upright to prevent the batter from spilling out. Fill the soufflé cups half full.

6. Bake cupcakes for 19 minutes. They are done when you can apply light pressure to the top of the cupcake and it bounces back. Also watch for a shiny part in the center of the cupcakes; if there is shine, they have not cooked long enough.

PRO TIP: *It is important to use Dutch-process cocoa in this recipe. The normal grocery store variety of cocoa is usually unsweetened but it has not been treated with an alkali to neutralize its natural acidity.*

---

2 cups heavy whipping cream
2 cups Guittard Extra-Dark Chocolate Chips (62 percent cacao)

DARK CHOCOLATE GANACHE FROSTING

Frosts 25 to 30 cupcakes

NOTE: *Make this frosting the day before you plan on using it, then whip it right before you need it. It really does need to sit overnight and there is no way to rush it.*

1. Pour the cream in a mixing bowl, and place the bowl over a pan of simmering water. Heat the cream until it starts to boil and climb the sides of the bowl. Watch it closely: when the cream starts to rise, it can very easily boil over.

2. Carefully remove the mixing bowl from the simmering water. Add the chocolate chips to the cream and let rest for about 5 minutes. Using a whisk, blend the cream and chocolate until the chocolate is fully incorporated. There should be no bits of chocolate left on the whisk.

3. Cover and refrigerate overnight or longer, up to one week.

chocolate • 33

4. When ready to use, place the mixing bowl back onto your mixer and use the flat paddle attachment to beat the chocolate. Start on low and gradually increase the speed until you see a ridge start to form around the paddle and the chocolate gets stiff. Scrape down the sides of the bowl often. Make sure you do not overbeat the chocolate. If you beat it past seeing ridges and stiffness, it will become grainy.

1 cup dark chocolate or chocolate bark pieces

DECORATIVE CHOCOLATE DISCS

Makes about 12 discs

1. Melt chocolate in a glass bowl in the microwave or in a metal bowl over a pan of simmering water, stirring frequently. When chocolate is melted and smooth, use a teaspoon and pour a small amount on a chilled flat baking sheet lined with parchment paper. Repeat with remaining melted chocolate. Place in refrigerator and chill. Use discs to decorate the top of cupcakes.

Assembly

Using a piping bag, frost each cupcake and top with chocolate chips. Drizzle melted chocolate over the top.

Twisted Sister

Mini's Chocoholic Cupcakes
Dark Chocolate Ganache Frosting
Salted Caramel Filling
Rock salt and mini pretzels for decoration

Makes 30 cupcakes in perfectly cute 2-ounce soufflé cups

chocolate ingredients

- ½ cup Guittard Extra-Dark Chocolate Chips, at least 62 percent cacao
- ½ cup boiling water, strong coffee, or espresso

wet ingredients

- ½ cup unsweetened applesauce
- ½ cup soybean oil
- 2 large eggs
- 1 tablespoon vanilla

dry ingredients

- 1½ cups unbleached flour
- 1 cup sugar
- 1 tablespoon baking powder
- ½ teaspoon salt
- ½ cup Dutch-process cocoa powder

MINI'S CHOCOHOLIC CUPCAKES

BEFORE YOU START: *Preheat oven to 350 degrees F.*

Place 30 soufflé cups on a flat baking sheet lined with parchment paper or a Silpat.

Place an 18-inch pastry bag with tip inside a large cup with the outside edge hanging over. You will use this to fill the soufflé cups with cupcake batter.

1. In a large glass measuring cup, combine the chocolate and boiling water. Let the chocolate melt in the hot liquid, then stir to combine and set aside.

2. Place all wet ingredients together in a mixing bowl. Mix on low speed with a wire whisk attachment for about 1 minute until all ingredients are blended. Slowly pour the warm chocolate mixture down the side of the bowl while the mixer is on low. Do not add the hot water and chocolate too quickly or you will cook the eggs.

3. Combine all dry ingredients in a separate bowl and stir with a spoon to combine.

4. Add dry ingredients to wet ingredients and blend on low speed for 30 seconds until combined. Batter will be lumpy. Scrape down the bowl and turn your mixer on high for

Twisted Sister continued

30 seconds. Scrape down bowl again, and return to high for another 30 seconds.

5. Pour batter into prepared pastry bag, then carefully pick up bag and hold the tip upright to prevent the batter from spilling out. Fill the soufflé cups half full.

6. Bake cupcakes for 19 minutes. They are done when you can apply light pressure to the top of the cupcake and it bounces back. Also watch for a shiny part in the center of the cupcakes; if there is shine, they have not cooked long enough.

PRO TIP: *It is important to use Dutch-process cocoa in this recipe. The normal grocery store variety of cocoa is usually unsweetened but it has not been treated with an alkali to neutralize its natural acidity.*

---

2 cups heavy whipping cream
2 cups Guittard Extra-Dark Chocolate Chips (62 percent cacao)

DARK CHOCOLATE GANACHE FROSTING

Frosts 25 to 30 cupcakes

NOTE: *Make this frosting the day before you plan on using it, then whip it right before you need it. It really does need to sit overnight and there is no way to rush it.*

1. Pour the cream in a mixing bowl, and place the bowl over a pan of simmering water. Heat the cream until it starts to boil and climb the sides of the bowl. Watch it closely: when the cream starts to rise it can very easily boil over.

2. Carefully remove the mixing bowl from the simmering water. Add the chocolate chips to the cream and let rest for about 5 minutes. Using a whisk, blend the cream and

chocolate until the chocolate is fully incorporated. There should be no bits of chocolate left on the whisk.

3. Cover and refrigerate overnight or longer, up to one week.

4. When ready to use, place the mixing bowl back onto your mixer and use the flat paddle attachment to beat the chocolate. Start on low and gradually increase the speed until you see a ridge start to form around the paddle and the chocolate gets stiff. Scrape down the sides of the bowl often. Make sure you do not overbeat the chocolate. If you beat it past seeing ridges and stiffness, it will become grainy.

SALTED CARAMEL FILLING

2	cups granulated sugar
1/4	cup unsalted butter
1/2	cup heavy cream
1	teaspoon rock salt

Fills 25 to 30 cupcakes

1. Place a heavy-duty wide-bottom saucepan over high heat and let the pan heat up while dry. When the pan is very hot, add the sugar to the pan; let the sugar melt from the heat, stirring occasionally with a wooden spoon. You may need to turn down the heat to prevent overcooking. The sugar will start to caramelize and turn a golden brown. Make sure that you scrape down the sides of the pan so all the granules of sugar are melted. Continue to cook the sugar until it changes to a light amber color and is very bubbly.

2. Reduce the heat to medium; add the butter to the melted sugar and stir until combined. Add the heavy cream and rock salt. Stir until combined, then return the heat to high.

3. Continue cooking the caramel until it becomes a medium amber color and you can drag your finger across the back

Twisted Sister
continued

of the spoon and the caramel does not fill in the gap. Use squeeze bottles to store and fill cupcakes.

Assembly

After cupcakes have cooled, use an apple corer to remove the center from each cupcake. Squeeze the Salted Caramel Filling inside each cupcake and frost with Dark Chocolate Ganache Frosting. Sprinkle rock salt on each cupcake and top with a pretzel. Drizzle more Salted Caramel on top.

Cookie Monster

Mini's Chocoholic Cupcakes
White Chocolate Ganache Frosting
Crushed and whole sandwich cookies for decoration

Makes 30 cupcakes in perfectly cute 2-ounce soufflé cups

chocolate ingredients

- ½ cup Guittard Extra-Dark Chocolate Chips, at least 62 percent cacao
- ½ cup boiling water, strong coffee, or espresso

wet ingredients

- ½ cup unsweetened applesauce
- ½ cup soybean oil
- 2 large eggs
- 1 tablespoon vanilla

dry ingredients

- 1½ cups unbleached flour
- 1 cup sugar
- 1 tablespoon baking powder
- ½ teaspoon salt
- ½ cup Dutch-process cocoa powder

MINI'S CHOCOHOLIC CUPCAKES

BEFORE YOU START: *Preheat oven to 350 degrees F.*

Place 30 soufflé cups on a flat baking sheet lined with parchment paper or a Silpat.

Place an 18-inch pastry bag with tip inside a large cup with the outside edge hanging over. You will use this to fill the soufflé cups with cupcake batter.

1. In a large glass measuring cup, combine the chocolate and boiling water. Let the chocolate melt in the hot liquid, then stir to combine and set aside.

2. Place all wet ingredients together in a mixing bowl. Mix on low speed with a wire whisk attachment for about 1 minute until all ingredients are blended. Slowly pour the warm chocolate mixture down the side of the bowl while the mixer is on low. Do not add the hot water and chocolate too quickly or you will cook the eggs.

3. Combine all dry ingredients in a separate bowl and stir with a spoon to combine.

4. Add dry ingredients to wet ingredients and blend on low speed for 30 seconds until combined. Batter will be lumpy. Scrape down the bowl and turn your mixer on high for 30 seconds. Scrape down bowl again, and return to high for another 30 seconds.

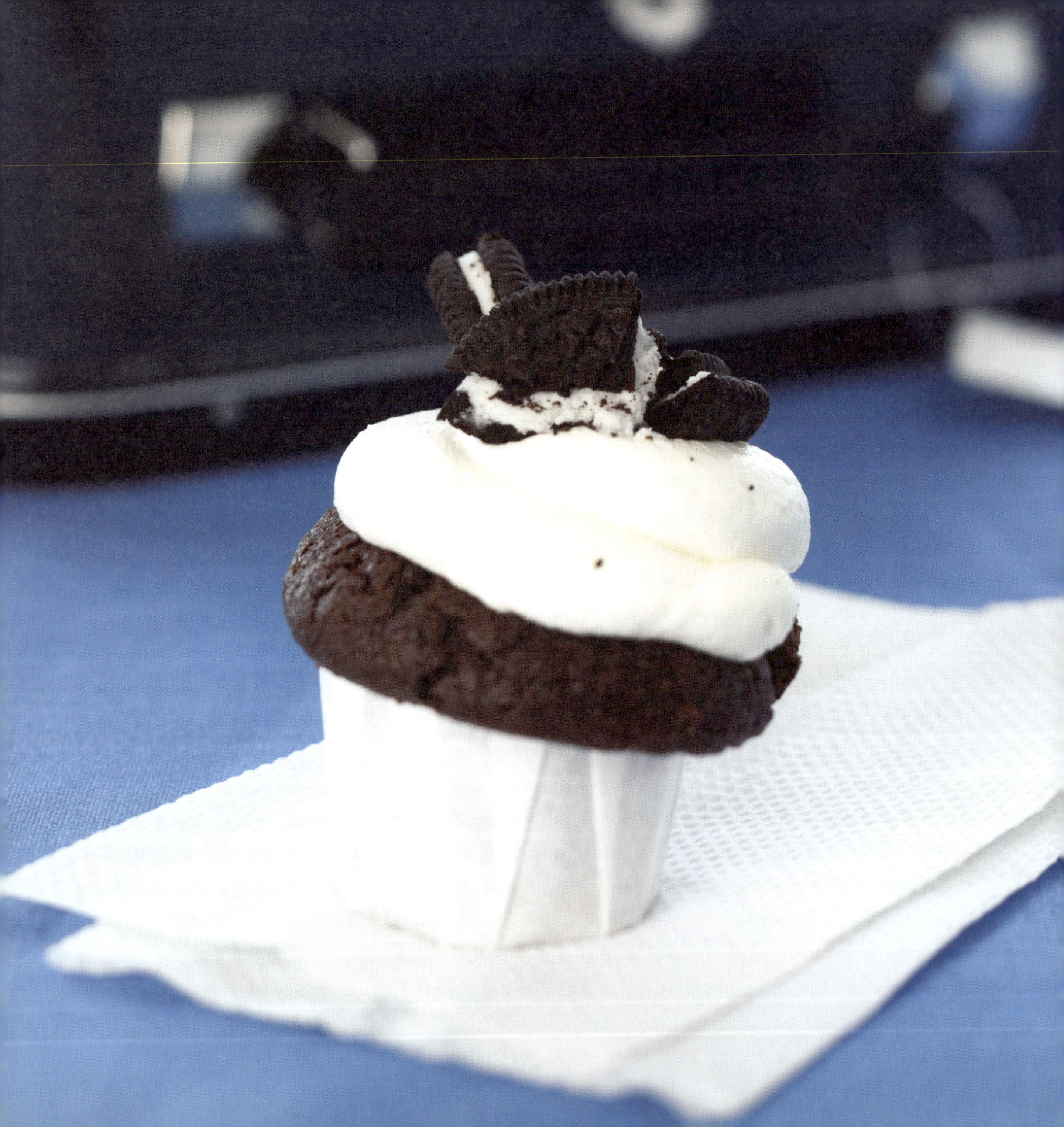

Cookie Monster
continued

5. Pour batter into prepared pastry bag, then carefully pick up bag and hold the tip upright to prevent the batter from spilling out. Fill the soufflé cups half full.

6. Bake cupcakes for 19 minutes. They are done when you can apply light pressure to the top of the cupcake and it bounces back. Also watch for a shiny part in the center of the cupcakes; if there is shine, they have not cooked long enough.

PRO TIP: *It is important to use Dutch-process cocoa in this recipe. The normal grocery store variety of cocoa is usually unsweetened but it has not been treated with an alkali to neutralize its natural acidity.*

---

2 cups heavy whipping cream
4 cups Guittard White Chocolate Chips

WHITE CHOCOLATE GANACHE FROSTING

Frosts 25 to 30 cupcakes

NOTE: *Make this frosting the day before you plan on using it, then whip it right before you need it. It really does need to sit overnight and there is no way to rush it.*

1. Pour the cream in a mixing bowl, and place the bowl over a pan of simmering water. Heat the cream until it starts to boil and climb the sides of the bowl. Watch it closely: when the cream starts to rise, it can very easily boil over.

2. Carefully remove the mixing bowl from the simmering water. Add the chocolate chips to the cream and let rest for about 5 minutes. Using a whisk, blend the cream and chocolate until the chocolate is fully incorporated. There should be no bits of chocolate left on the whisk.

Cookie Monster
continued

3. Cover and refrigerate the chocolate overnight or longer, up to one week.

4. When ready to use, place the mixing bowl back onto your mixer and use the flat paddle attachment to beat the chocolate. Start on low and gradually increase the speed until you see a ridge start to form around the paddle and the chocolate gets stiff. Scrape down the sides of the bowl often. Make sure you do not overbeat the chocolate. If you beat it past seeing ridges and stiffness, it will become grainy.

Assembly

After your cupcakes have cooled, frost each cupcake with White Chocolate Ganache Frosting and top with crushed or whole sandwich cookies.

Mini's Sweet and Salty

Mini's Buttery Vanilla Cupcakes
Peanut Butter Frosting
Salted Caramel Filling
Dark Chocolate Ganache Frosting
Salted peanuts for decoration

Makes 30 cupcakes in perfectly cute 2-ounce soufflé cups

wet ingredients

- ¼ cup sour cream
- ¼ cup buttermilk
- ½ cup unsweetened applesauce
- ½ cup soybean oil
- ¼ cup unsalted butter, room temperature
- 2 large eggs
- 1 egg yolk
- 2 tablespoons vanilla
- 1 tablespoon vanilla bean paste

dry ingredients

- 2 cups unbleached flour
- 1 cup sugar
- 1¼ tablespoons baking powder
- ½ teaspoon salt

MINI'S BUTTERY VANILLA CUPCAKES

BEFORE YOU START: *Preheat oven to 350 degrees F.*

Place 30 soufflé cups on a flat baking sheet lined with parchment paper or a Silpat.

Place an 18-inch pastry bag with tip inside a large cup with the outside edge hanging over. You will use this to fill the soufflé cups with cupcake batter.

1. Place all wet ingredients together in a mixing bowl. Mix on low speed with a wire whisk attachment for about 1 minute until all ingredients are blended.

2. Combine all dry ingredients in a separate bowl and stir with a spoon to combine.

3. Add dry ingredients to wet ingredients and blend on low for 1 minute until combined. Batter will be lumpy but blended. Scrape down the sides of the bowl. Turn mixer on high for 30 seconds; most of the lumps will disappear and small air bubbles will start to form.

4. Pour batter into prepared pastry bag, then carefully pick up bag and hold the tip upright to prevent the batter from spilling out. Fill the soufflé cups half full.

5. Bake for 17 minutes. Cupcakes are done when you can apply light pressure to the top of the cupcake and it bounces back.

Mini's Sweet and Salty
continued

- 2 cups granulated sugar
- ¼ cup unsalted butter
- ½ cup heavy cream
- 1 teaspoon rock salt

SALTED CARAMEL FILLING

Fills 25 to 30 cupcakes

1. Place a heavy-duty wide-bottom saucepan over high heat and let the pan heat up while dry. When the pan is very hot, add the sugar to the pan; let the sugar melt from the heat, stirring occasionally with a wooden spoon. You may need to turn down the heat to prevent overcooking. The sugar will start to caramelize and turn a golden brown. Make sure that you scrape down the sides of the pan so all the granules of sugar are melted. Continue to cook the sugar until it changes to a light amber color and is very bubbly.

2. Reduce the heat to medium; add the butter to the melted sugar and stir until combined. Add the heavy cream and rock salt. Stir until combined, then return the heat to high.

3. Continue cooking the caramel until it becomes a medium amber color and you can drag your finger across the back of the spoon and the caramel does not fill in the gap. Use squeeze bottles to store and fill cupcakes.

- ½ cup unsalted butter, room temperature
- ½ cup creamy peanut butter
- 1 cup powdered sugar

PEANUT BUTTER FROSTING

Fills 25 to 30 cupcakes

1. In a mixing bowl with a wire whisk attachment, beat the butter and peanut butter for 3 to 4 minutes. Continually scrape down sides of bowl to ensure all the butter is creamy and well blended.

2. Add the powdered sugar, ½ cup at a time, to the butter mixture. Mix in each addition of the powdered sugar completely, as this will eliminate lumps. Scrape down the bowl often.

2 cups heavy whipping cream
2 cups Guittard Extra-Dark Chocolate Chips (62 percent cacao)

DARK CHOCOLATE GANACHE FROSTING

Frosts 25 to 30 cupcakes

NOTE: *Make this frosting the day before you plan on using it, then whip it right before you need it. It really does need to sit overnight and there is no way to rush it.*

1. Pour the cream in a mixing bowl, and place the bowl over a pan of simmering water. Heat the cream until it starts to boil and climb the sides of the bowl. Watch it closely: when the cream starts to rise it can very easily boil over.

2. Carefully remove the mixing bowl from the boiling water. Add the chocolate chips to the cream and let rest for about 5 minutes. Using a whisk, blend the cream and chocolate until the chocolate is fully incorporated. There should be no bits of chocolate left on the whisk.

3. Cover and refrigerate overnight or longer, up to one week.

4. When ready to use, place the mixing bowl back onto your mixer and use the flat paddle attachment to beat the chocolate. Start on low and gradually increase the speed until you see a ridge start to form around the paddle and the chocolate gets stiff. Scrape down the sides of the bowl often. Make sure you do not overbeat the chocolate. If you beat it past seeing ridges and stiffness, it will become grainy.

Assembly

After your cupcakes have cooled, core each cupcake with an apple corer, fill with a combination of Peanut Butter Frosting and Salted Caramel Filling. Frost each cupcake with Dark Chocolate Ganache Frosting; top with salted peanuts and a caramel drizzle.

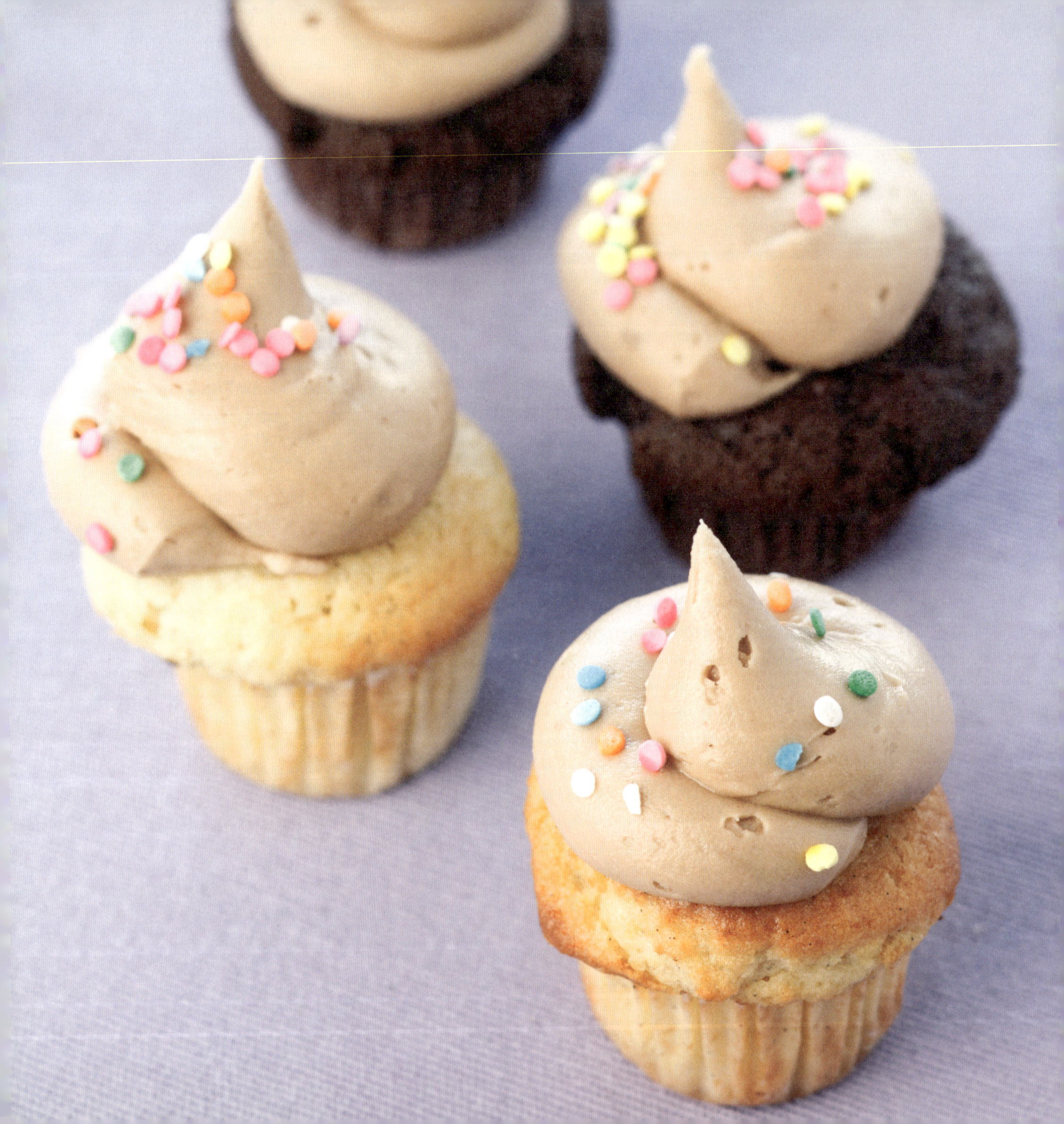

"CHIP's" The Ponch and Jon

Mini's Buttery Vanilla Cupcakes
Milk Chocolate Buttercream
  Frosting
Candy dots for decoration

Makes 30 cupcakes in perfectly cute 2-ounce soufflé cups

VARIATION

Use Mini's Chocoholic Cupcakes (see page 49)

wet ingredients

- ¼ cup sour cream
- ¼ cup buttermilk
- ½ cup unsweetened applesauce
- ½ cup soybean oil
- ¼ cup unsalted butter, room temperature
- 2 large eggs
- 1 egg yolk
- 2 tablespoons vanilla
- 1 tablespoon vanilla bean paste

dry ingredients

- 2 cups unbleached flour
- 1 cup sugar
- 1¼ tablespoons baking powder
- ½ teaspoon salt

MINI'S BUTTERY VANILLA CUPCAKES

BEFORE YOU START: *Preheat oven to 350 degrees F.*

Place 30 soufflé cups on a flat baking sheet lined with parchment paper or a Silpat.

Place an 18-inch pastry bag with tip inside a large cup with the outside edge hanging over. You will use this to fill the soufflé cups with cupcake batter.

1. Place all wet ingredients together in a mixing bowl. Mix on low speed with a wire whisk attachment for about 1 minute until all ingredients are blended.

2. Combine all dry ingredients in a separate bowl and stir with a spoon to combine.

3. Add dry ingredients to wet ingredients and blend on low for 1 minute until combined. Batter will be lumpy but blended. Scrape down the sides of the bowl. Turn mixer on high for 30 seconds; most of the lumps will disappear and small air bubbles will start to form.

4. Pour batter into prepared pastry bag, then carefully pick up bag and hold the tip upright to prevent the batter from spilling out. Fill the soufflé cups half full.

"CHIP's" The Ponch and Jon continued

5. Bake for 17 minutes. Cupcakes are done when you can apply light pressure to the top of the cupcake and it bounces back.

- 5 egg whites, room temperature
- 1⅛ cups granulated sugar
- Pinch salt
- 1 teaspoon vanilla
- 2 cups unsalted butter, room temperature
- ½ cup melted Guittard Extra-Dark Chocolate Chips (62 percent cacao)
- 2 cups powdered sugar

MILK CHOCOLATE BUTTERCREAM FROSTING

Frosts 25 to 30 cupcakes

1. In a mixing bowl, whisk egg whites, sugar, and salt. Place the mixing bowl over a pan of simmering water. Whisk the mixture every couple of minutes to ensure the sugar granules along the side of the bowl are fully melted with the egg. Continue to whisk until temperature reaches 174 degrees F.

2. Remove bowl from the pan of simmering water and use wire whisk to beat the mixture on high until the bottom of the bowl no longer retains any heat and the mixture reaches a stiff peak consistency. Add vanilla; whisk until incorporated.

3. Remove the wire whisk and use the paddle attachment to finish the frosting. With the mixer set on medium-low, add the butter, 1 tablespoon at a time, waiting until each addition of butter is blended in before adding the next. If the frosting becomes curdled, do not worry; just continue to add the butter and beat the frosting, and it will eventually become creamy and smooth.

4. Once all the butter is incorporated and the mixture is creamy and smooth, slowly pour in the melted chocolate and rewhip. Add the powdered sugar, ½ cup at a time. Continue until all sugar is incorporated. Frosting will be slightly stiff.

Assembly

After your cupcakes have cooled, frost each cupcake with Milk Chocolate Buttercream Frosting and top with candy dots.

PB Fix

Mini's Chocoholic Cupcakes
Peanut Butter Frosting
Salted peanuts for decoration
Chocolate discs for decoration
  (optional, see page 33)

Makes 30 cupcakes in perfectly cute 2-ounce soufflé cups

chocolate ingredients

- ½ cup Guittard Extra-Dark Chocolate Chips, at least 62 percent cacao
- ½ cup boiling water, strong coffee, or espresso

wet ingredients

- ½ cup unsweetened applesauce
- ½ cup soybean oil
- 2 large eggs
- 1 tablespoon vanilla

dry ingredients

- 1½ cups unbleached flour
- 1 cup sugar
- 1 tablespoon baking powder
- ½ teaspoon salt
- ½ cup Dutch-process cocoa powder

MINI'S CHOCOHOLIC CUPCAKES

BEFORE YOU START: *Preheat oven to 350 degrees F.*

Place 30 soufflé cups on a flat baking sheet lined with parchment paper or a Silpat.

Place an 18-inch pastry bag with tip inside a large cup with the outside edge hanging over. You will use this to fill the soufflé cups with cupcake batter.

1. In a large glass measuring cup, combine the chocolate and boiling water. Let the chocolate melt in the hot liquid, then stir to combine and set aside.

2. Place all wet ingredients together in a mixing bowl. Mix on low speed with a wire whisk attachment for about 1 minute until all ingredients are blended. Slowly pour the warm chocolate mixture down the side of the bowl while the mixer is on low. Do not add the hot water and chocolate too quickly or you will cook the eggs.

3. Put all dry ingredients in a separate bowl and stir with a spoon to combine.

4. Add dry ingredients to wet ingredients and blend on low speed for 30 seconds until combined. Batter will be lumpy. Scrape down the bowl and turn your mixer on high for 30 seconds. Scrape down bowl again, and return to high for another 30 seconds.

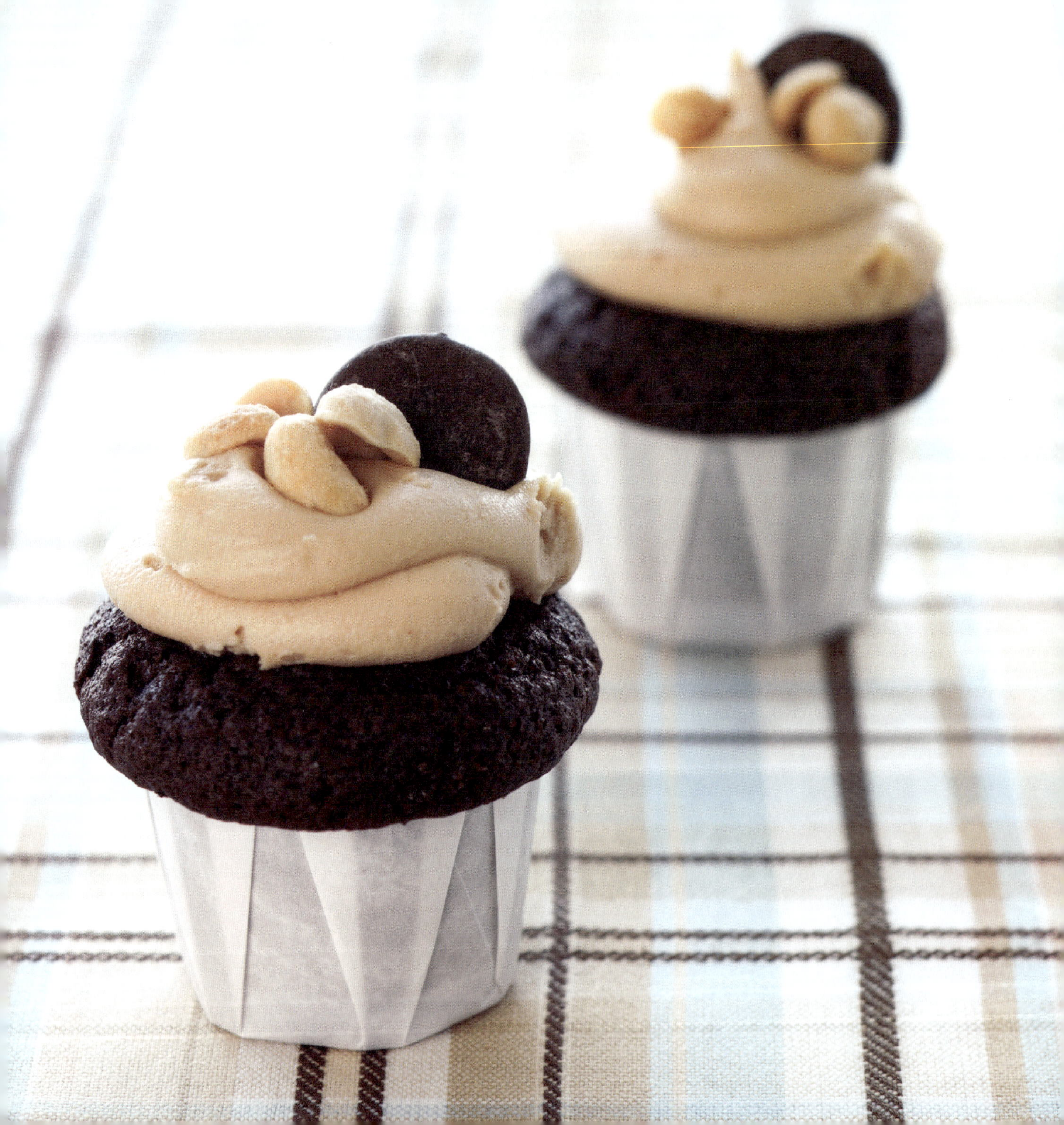

PB Fix
continued

5. Pour batter into prepared pastry bag, then carefully pick up bag and hold the tip upright to prevent the batter from spilling out. Fill the soufflé cups half full.

6. Bake cupcakes for 19 minutes. They are done when you can apply light pressure to the top of the cupcake and it bounces back. Also watch for a shiny part in the center of the cupcakes; if there is shine, they have not cooked long enough.

PRO TIP: *It is important to use Dutch-process cocoa in this recipe. The normal grocery store variety of cocoa is usually unsweetened but it has not been treated with an alkali to neutralize its natural acidity.*

½ cup unsalted butter, room temperature
½ cup creamy peanut butter
1 cup powdered sugar

PEANUT BUTTER FROSTING

Frosts 25 to 30 cupcakes

1. In a mixing bowl with a wire whisk attachment, beat the butter and peanut butter for 3 to 4 minutes. Continually scrape down sides of bowl to ensure all the butter is creamy and well blended.

2. Add the powdered sugar, ½ cup at a time, to the butter mixture. Mix in each addition of the powdered sugar completely, as this will eliminate lumps. Scrape down the bowl often.

Assembly
After your cupcakes have cooled, frost each cupcake with Peanut Butter Frosting and top with salted peanuts and a chocolate disc, if using.

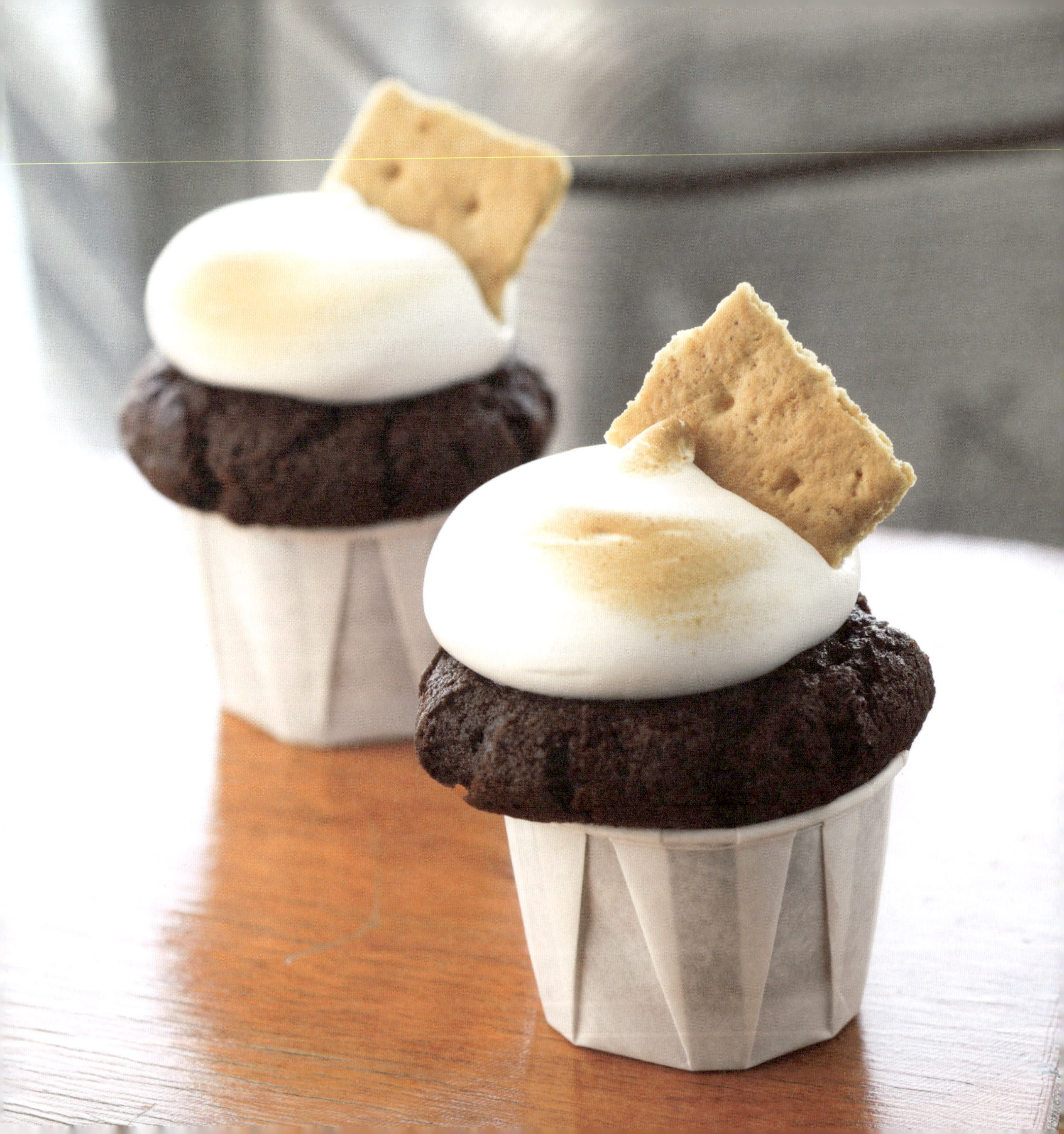

S'Mores Please

Mini's Chocoholic Cupcakes
Mini's Matterhorn Frosting
Graham crackers for decoration

Makes 30 cupcakes in perfectly cute 2-ounce soufflé cups

chocolate ingredients

- ½ cup Guittard Extra-Dark Chocolate Chips, at least 62 percent cacao
- ½ cup boiling water, strong coffee, or espresso

wet ingredients

- ½ cup unsweetened applesauce
- ½ cup soybean oil
- 2 large eggs
- 1 tablespoon vanilla

dry ingredients

- 1½ cups unbleached flour
- 1 cup sugar
- 1 tablespoon baking powder
- ½ teaspoon salt
- ½ cup Dutch-process cocoa powder

MINI'S CHOCOHOLIC CUPCAKES

BEFORE YOU START: *Preheat oven to 350 degrees F.*

Place 30 soufflé cups on a flat baking sheet lined with parchment paper or a Silpat.

Place an 18-inch pastry bag with tip inside a large cup with the outside edge hanging over. You will use this to fill the soufflé cups with cupcake batter.

1. In a large glass measuring cup, combine the chocolate and boiling water. Let the chocolate melt in the hot liquid, then stir to combine and set aside.

2. Place all wet ingredients together in a mixing bowl. Mix on low speed with a wire whisk attachment for about 1 minute until all ingredients are blended. Slowly pour the warm chocolate mixture down the side of the bowl while the mixer is on low. Do not add the hot water and chocolate too quickly or you will cook the eggs.

3. Put all dry ingredients in a separate bowl and stir with a spoon to combine.

4. Add dry ingredients to wet ingredients and blend on low speed for 30 seconds until combined. Batter will be lumpy. Scrape down the bowl and turn your mixer on high for 30 seconds. Scrape down bowl again, and return to high for another 30 seconds.

S'Mores Please
continued

5. Pour batter into prepared pastry bag, then carefully pick up bag and hold the tip upright to prevent the batter from spilling out. Fill the soufflé cups half full.

6. Bake cupcakes for 19 minutes. They are done when you can apply light pressure to the top of the cupcake and it bounces back. Also watch for a shiny part in the center of the cupcakes; if there is shine, they have not cooked long enough.

PRO TIP: *It is important to use Dutch-process cocoa in this recipe. The normal grocery store variety of cocoa is usually unsweetened but it has not been treated with an alkali to neutralize its natural acidity.*

½ cup egg whites, room temperature
½ cup light corn syrup
½ cup granulated sugar
1 teaspoon vanilla

MINI'S MATTERHORN FROSTING

Frosts 25 to 30 cupcakes

Okay, it's really a Swiss meringue but when finished and on top of a cupcake it reminds me of the Matterhorn at Disneyland.

1. Place egg whites, corn syrup, and sugar into a mixing bowl and whisk together. Place mixing bowl over a pan of simmering water to double boil. Occasionally whisk the mixture to prevent the egg whites from cooking separately from the sugars. The mixture is ready when the temperature reaches 174 degrees F. This will destroy harmful bacteria.

2. Carefully remove the mixing bowl form the hot steam and attach the bowl to your mixer.

3. Using the whisk attachment, beat on low for about 2 minutes, then slowly raise the speed of the mixer until

it is on high. Mix until dense soft peaks form. At this point add the vanilla and rewhip until combined.

4. It's best to use this frosting right after it is made; if you do not use it all, store it in your refrigerator for up to a week and rewhip it prior to using.

PRO TIP: *Make sure when you separate the egg whites you do not have any yolk in the whites. The fat from the yolk will prevent the whites from whipping.*

PRO TIP: *Use a towel to put the mixing bowl onto your mixer, as the edges will be very hot from the steam.*

Assembly

After your cupcakes have cooled, frost each one with Mini's Matterhorn Frosting, brown using a small kitchen torch, and top with graham crackers.

Southern Comfort

Mini's Red Velvet Cupcakes
Mini's Cream Cheese Frosting
Crushed pecans for decoration

Makes 30 cupcakes in perfectly cute 2-ounce soufflé cups

wet ingredients

- ½ cup buttermilk
- 1 cup unsweetened applesauce
- ¾ cup soybean oil
- ¾ cup puréed beets
- 2 eggs
- 2 tablespoons vanilla
- 1 tablespoon champagne vinegar

dry ingredients

- 2 cups unbleached flour
- 1 cup sugar
- 2 tablespoons baking powder
- ½ cup Dutch-process cocoa powder
- ½ teaspoon salt

MINI'S RED VELVET CUPCAKES

BEFORE YOU START: *Preheat oven to 350 degrees F.*

Place 30 soufflé cups on a flat baking sheet lined with parchment paper or a Silpat.

Place an 18-inch pastry bag with tip inside a large cup with the outside edge hanging over. You will use this to fill the soufflé cups with cupcake batter.

1. Place all wet ingredients together in a mixing bowl. Mix on low speed with a wire whisk attachment for about 1 minute until all ingredients are blended.

2. Combine all dry ingredients in a separate bowl and stir with a spoon to combine.

3. Add dry ingredients to wet ingredients and blend on low speed for 30 seconds until combined. Batter will be lumpy. Scrape down the bowl and turn mixer on high for 30 seconds. Scrape down bowl again and return to high for another 30 seconds.

4. Pour batter into pastry bag, then carefully pick up bag and hold the tip upright to prevent the batter from spilling out. Fill the soufflé cups half full.

5. Bake cupcakes for 22 minutes. They are done when you can apply light pressure to the top of a cupcake and it bounces back. Also watch for a shiny part in the center

of the cupcakes; if there is shine, they have not cooked long enough.

PRO TIP: *Using puréed beets in this recipe eliminates the need for the large quantities of red food dye normally called for in traditional red velvet cakes. The beets add moisture and a nice earthy red color. They do not carry any beet taste into the cake.*

PRO TIP: *It is important to use Dutch-process cocoa in this recipe. The normal grocery store variety of cocoa is usually unsweetened but it has not been treated with an alkali to neutralize its natural acidity.*

MINI'S CREAM CHEESE FROSTING

- 1 (8-ounce) package cream cheese, room temperature
- 1 tablespoon vanilla
- 4 cups powdered sugar
- Food coloring (optional)

Frosts 25 to 30 cupcakes

1. In a mixing bowl with a wire whisk attachment, beat the cream cheese and vanilla for 3 to 4 minutes. Continually scrape down sides of bowl to ensure all the cream cheese is creamy and well blended.

2. Slowly add the powdered sugar, about $1/2$ cup at a time, to the mixture. If you are going to tint the frosting, add the food coloring about halfway through the powdered sugar addition. Mix in each addition of powdered sugar completely, as this will eliminate lumps. Scrape down the bowl often.

Assembly

After your cupcakes have cooled, frost each cupcake with Mini's Cream Cheese Frosting and top with crushed pecans.

FRUIT & CITRUS

Key Largo Pie
61

Lemon Pie
64

Mary Ann
67

Berry Lemon
71

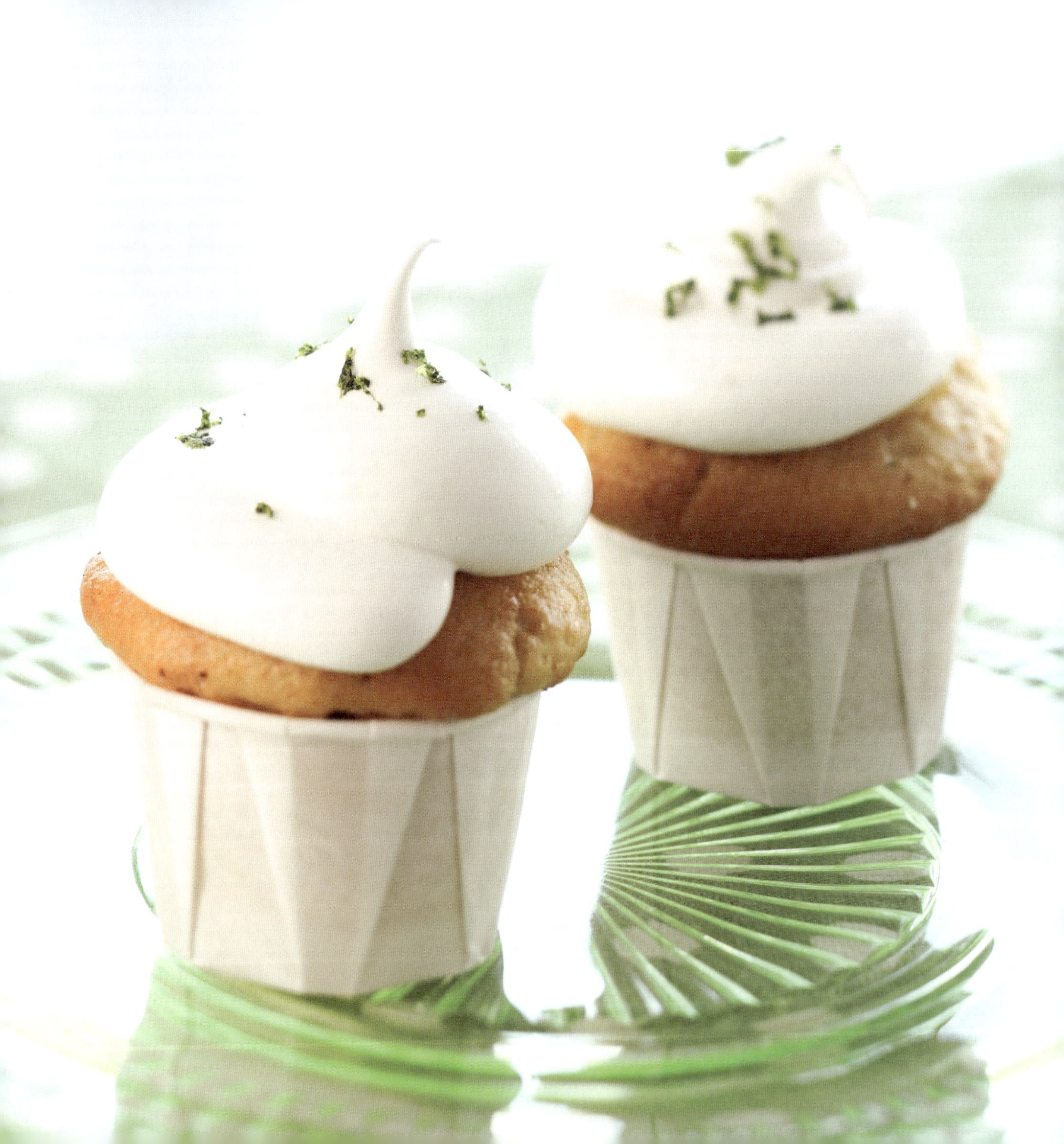

Key Largo Pie

- Key Largo Lime Cupcakes
- Key Lime Curd Filling
- Mini's Matterhorn Frosting
- Lime zest for decoration

Makes 30 cupcakes in perfectly cute 2-ounce soufflé cups

wet ingredients

- Zest of 5 Key limes
- Juice of 5 Key limes, with enough milk added to the lime juice to equal ¾ cup of liquid
- ¼ cup sour cream
- ½ cup unsweetened applesauce
- ½ cup soybean oil
- 3 eggs
- 2 tablespoons vanilla

dry ingredients

- 2½ cups unbleached flour
- 1½ cups sugar
- 1 tablespoon baking powder
- ½ teaspoon salt

KEY LARGO LIME CUPCAKES

BEFORE YOU START: *Preheat oven to 350 degrees F.*

Place 30 soufflé cups on a flat baking sheet lined with parchment paper or a Silpat.

Place an 18-inch pastry bag with tip inside a large cup with the outside edge hanging over. You will use this to fill the soufflé cups with cupcake batter.

1. Place all wet ingredients together in a mixing bowl. Mix on low speed with a wire whisk attachment for about 1 minute until all ingredients are blended.

2. Combine all dry ingredients in a separate bowl and stir with a spoon to combine.

3. Add dry ingredients to wet ingredients and blend on low speed for 15 seconds until combined. Batter will be lumpy. Scrape down the bowl and turn mixer on high for 30 seconds. Scrape down bowl again, and return to high for another 30 seconds.

4. Pour batter into prepared pastry bag, then carefully pick up bag and hold the tip upright to prevent the batter from spilling out. Fill the soufflé cups half full.

5. Bake cupcakes for 24 minutes. They are done when you can apply light pressure to the top of a cupcake and it bounces back.

Key Largo Pie
continued

PRO TIP: *Use Key limes in this recipe if you can. Key limes are much smaller but more intense in flavor than their cousins, the larger Persian variety.*

6	key limes
1	cup key lime juice
¾	cup granulated sugar
2	eggs
1	cup unsalted butter, room temperature

KEY LIME CURD FILLING

Fills 25 to 30 cupcakes

1. Zest the limes into a double boiler. Juice the limes into a glass measuring cup and then add enough key lime juice to equal 1 cup. Add lime juice, sugar, and eggs to the double boiler and whisk until egg mixture is thoroughly mixed with the lime juice and zest.

2. Cut butter into small pieces and add to mixture; whisk until butter is melted. Continue to whisk occasionally; the mixture will thicken slightly. This takes about 20 minutes.

3. Let the mixture cool in the fridge completely before using. As the lime curd cools, it will thicken even more. Use squeeze bottles to fill cupcakes and store up to 1 week.

½	cup egg whites, room temperature
½	cup light corn syrup
½	cup granulated sugar
1	teaspoon vanilla

MINI'S MATTERHORN FROSTING

Frosts 25 to 30 cupcakes

Okay, it's really a Swiss meringue but when finished and on top of a cupcake it reminds me of the Matterhorn at Disneyland.

1. Place egg whites, corn syrup, and sugar into a mixing bowl and whisk together. Place mixing bowl over a pan of simmering water to double boil. Occasionally whisk the

mixture to prevent the egg whites from cooking separately from the sugars. The mixture is ready when the temperature reaches 174 degrees F. This will destroy harmful bacteria.

2. Carefully remove the mixing bowl form the hot steam and attach the bowl to your mixer.

3. Using the whisk attachment, beat on low for about 2 minutes, then slowly raise the speed of the mixer until it is on high. Mix until dense soft peaks form. At this point add the vanilla and rewhip until combined.

4. It's best to use this frosting right after it is made; if you do not use it all, store it in your refrigerator for up to a week and rewhip it prior to using.

PRO TIP: *Make sure when you separate the egg whites you do not have any yolk in the whites. The fat from the yolk will prevent the whites from whipping.*

PRO TIP: *Use a towel to put the mixing bowl onto your mixer, as the edges will be very hot from the steam.*

Assembly

After the cupcakes have cooled, use an apple corer to remove the center from each cupcake. Squeeze the Key Lime Curd Filling inside each cupcake and frost with Mini's Matterhorn Frosting. Use a bit of lime zest on top of each cupcake for decoration.

Lemon Pie

Mini's Lemonicious Cupcakes
Lemon Curd Filling
Mini's Matterhorn Frosting

Makes 30 cupcakes in perfectly cute 2-ounce soufflé cups

wet ingredients

- Zest of 3 lemons
- Juice of 3 lemons, with enough milk added to the lemon juice to equal ¾ cup of liquid
- ¼ cup sour cream
- ½ cup unsweetened applesauce
- ¼ cup soybean oil
- ¼ cup unsalted butter, room temperature
- 3 eggs
- 2 tablespoons vanilla

dry ingredients

- 2½ cups unbleached flour
- 1½ cups sugar
- 2 tablespoons baking powder
- ½ teaspoon salt

MINI'S LEMONICIOUS CUPCAKES

BEFORE YOU START: *Preheat oven to 350 degrees F.*

Place 30 soufflé cups on a flat baking sheet lined with parchment paper or a Silpat.

Place an 18-inch pastry bag with tip inside a large cup with the outside edge hanging over. You will use this to fill the soufflé cups with cupcake batter.

1. Place all wet ingredients together in a mixing bowl. Mix on low speed with a wire whisk attachment for about 1 minute until all ingredients are blended.

2. Combine all dry ingredients in a separate bowl and stir with a spoon to combine.

3. Add dry ingredients to wet ingredients and blend on low speed for 15 seconds until combined. Batter will be lumpy. Scrape down the bowl and turn mixer on high for 30 seconds. Scrape down the bowl again, and return to high for another 30 seconds.

4. Pour batter into prepared pastry bag, then carefully pick up bag and hold the tip upright to prevent batter from spilling out. Fill the soufflé cups half full.

5. Bake cupcakes for 24 minutes. They are done when you can apply light pressure to the top of a cupcake and it bounces back.

LEMON CURD FILLING

- 3 lemons
- 1 cup lemon juice
- ½ cup granulated sugar
- 2 eggs
- 1 cup unsalted butter, room temperature

Fills 25 to 30 cupcakes

1. Zest the lemons into a double boiler. Juice the lemons into a glass measuring cup and then add enough lemon juice to equal 1 cup. Add lemon juice, sugar, and eggs to the double boiler and whisk until egg mixture is thoroughly mixed with the lemon juice and zest.

2. Cut butter into small pieces and add to mixture; whisk until butter is melted. Continue to whisk occasionally; the mixture will thicken slightly. This takes about 20 minutes.

3. Let the mixture cool in the fridge completely before using. As the lemon curd cools, it will thicken even more. Use squeeze bottles to fill cupcakes and store up to 1 week.

MINI'S MATTERHORN FROSTING

- ½ cup egg whites, room temperature
- ½ cup light corn syrup
- ½ cup granulated sugar
- 1 teaspoon vanilla

Frosts 25 to 30 cupcakes

Okay, it's really a Swiss meringue but when finished and on top of a cupcake it reminds me of the Matterhorn at Disneyland.

1. Place egg whites, corn syrup, and sugar into a mixing bowl and whisk together. Place mixing bowl over a pan of simmering water to double boil. Occasionally whisk the mixture to prevent the egg whites from cooking separately from the sugars. The mixture is ready when the temperature reaches 174 degrees F. This will destroy harmful bacteria.

2. Carefully remove the mixing bowl form the hot steam and attach the bowl to your mixer.

Lemon Pie continued

3. Using the whisk attachment, beat on low for about 2 minutes, then slowly raise the speed of the mixer until it is on high. Mix until dense soft peaks form. At this point add the vanilla and rewhip until combined.

4. It's best to use this frosting right after it is made; if you do not use it all, store it in your refrigerator for up to a week and rewhip it prior to using.

PRO TIP: *Make sure when you separate the egg whites you do not have any yolk in the whites. The fat from the yolk will prevent the whites from whipping.*

PRO TIP: *Use a towel to put the mixing bowl onto your mixer, as the edges will be very hot from the steam.*

Assembly

After the cupcakes have cooled, use an apple corer to remove the center from each cupcake. Squeeze the Lemon Curd Filling inside each cupcake and frost with Mini's Matterhorn Frosting. Brown each cupcake with a kitchen torch.

… fruit & citrus • 67

Mary Ann

Mini's Buttery Vanilla Cupcakes
Banana Cream Filling
Matterhorn Buttercream Frosting
Toasted coconut for decoration

Makes 30 cupcakes in perfectly cute 2-ounce soufflé cups

wet ingredients

- ¼ cup sour cream
- ¼ cup buttermilk
- ½ cup unsweetened applesauce
- ½ cup soybean oil
- ¼ cup unsalted butter, room temperature
- 2 large eggs
- 1 egg yolk
- 2 tablespoons vanilla
- 1 tablespoon vanilla bean paste

dry ingredients

- 2 cups unbleached flour
- 1 cup sugar
- 1¼ tablespoons baking powder
- ½ teaspoon salt

MINI'S BUTTERY VANILLA CUPCAKES

BEFORE YOU START: *Preheat oven to 350 degrees F.*

Place 30 soufflé cups on a flat baking sheet lined with parchment paper or a Silpat.

Place an 18-inch pastry bag with tip inside a large cup with the outside edge hanging over. You will use this to fill the soufflé cups with cupcake batter.

1. Place all wet ingredients together in a mixing bowl. Mix on low speed with a wire whisk attachment for about 1 minute until all ingredients are blended.

2. Combine all dry ingredients in a separate bowl and stir with a spoon to combine.

3. Add dry ingredients to wet ingredients and blend on low for 1 minute until combined. Batter will be lumpy but blended. Scrape down the sides of the bowl. Turn mixer on high for 30 seconds; most of the lumps will disappear and small air bubbles will start to form.

4. Pour batter into prepared pastry bag, then carefully pick up bag and hold the tip upright to prevent the batter from spilling out. Fill the soufflé cups half full.

5. Bake for 17 minutes. Cupcakes are done when you can apply light pressure to the top of the cupcake and it bounces back.

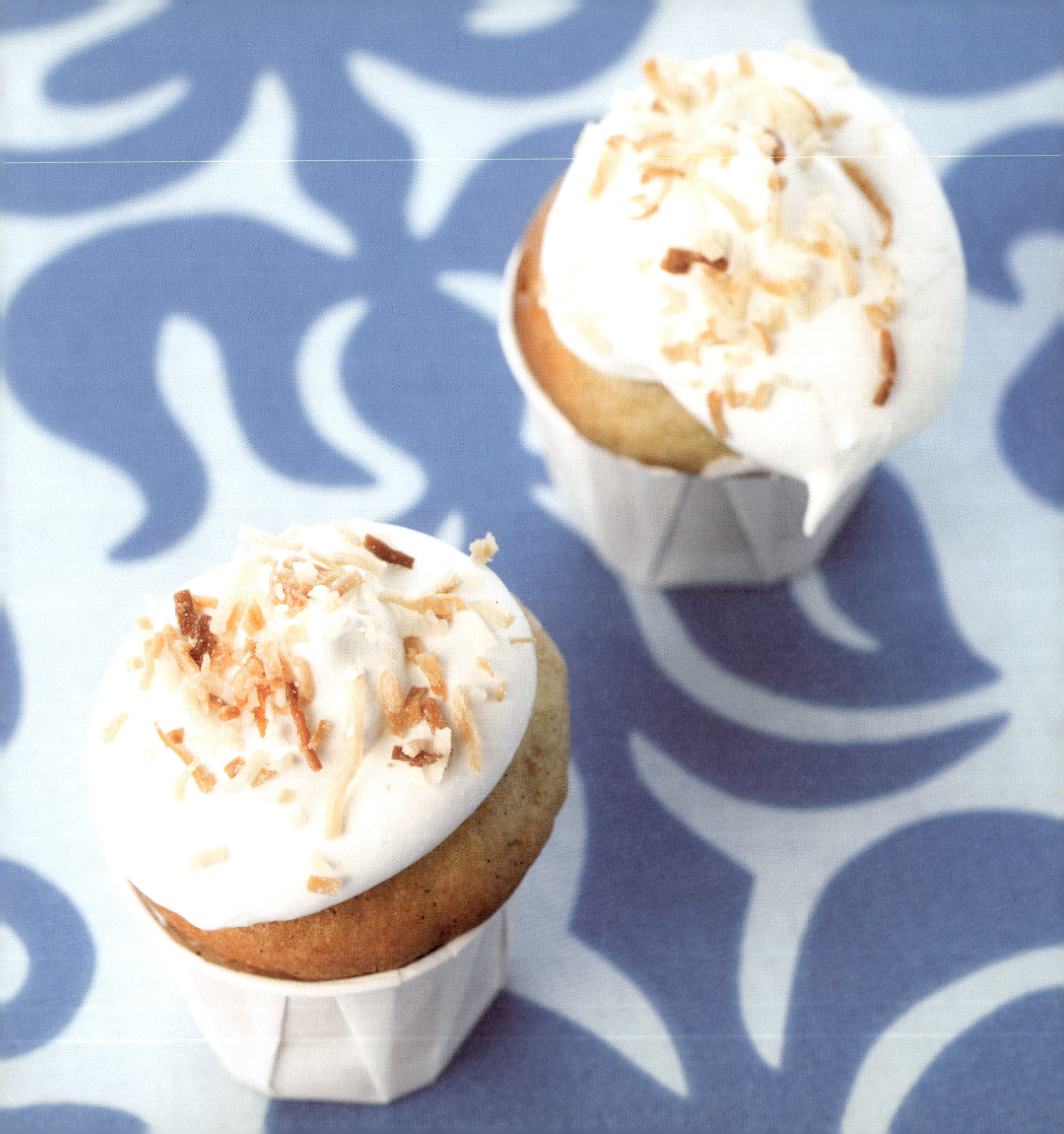

Mary Ann
continued

- 1 cup scalded milk
- 3 egg yolks
- 3 ripe bananas
- ½ cup granulated sugar
- 1 teaspoon vanilla
- 1 tablespoon unsalted butter
- ⅛ cup flour

BANANA CREAM FILLING

Fills 25 to 30 cupcakes

1. While milk is heating in a saucepan, combine egg yolks, bananas, sugar, vanilla, and butter in a bowl. Whisk on high until light and creamy. Add flour and whisk again.

2. Slowly add ½ cup of hot milk to banana mixture while mixing on low. Continue adding milk slowly until all the milk is added and blended. Return mixture to saucepan and cook over medium heat until thick and bubbly.

3. Let mixture cool in fridge before using. Use squeeze bottles to store and fill cupcakes.

- ½ cup egg whites, room temperature
- ½ cup light corn syrup
- ½ cup granulated sugar
- 1 teaspoon vanilla

MINI'S MATTERHORN FROSTING

Frosts 25 to 30 cupcakes

Okay, it's really a Swiss meringue but when finished and on top of a cupcake it reminds me of the Matterhorn at Disneyland.

1. Place egg whites, corn syrup, and sugar into a mixing bowl and whisk together. Place mixing bowl over a pan of simmering water to double boil. Occasionally whisk the mixture to prevent the egg whites from cooking separately from the sugars. The mixture is ready when the temperature reaches 174 degrees F. This will destroy harmful bacteria.

2. Carefully remove the mixing bowl form the hot steam and attach the bowl to your mixer.

3. Using the whisk attachment, beat on low for about 2 minutes, then slowly raise the speed of the mixer until

Mary Ann continued

it is on high. Mix until dense soft peaks form. At this point add the vanilla and rewhip until combined.

4. It's best to use this frosting right after it is made; if you do not use it all, store it in your refrigerator for up to a week and rewhip it prior to using.

PRO TIP: *Make sure when you separate the egg whites you do not have any yolk in the whites. The fat from the yolk will prevent the whites from whipping.*

PRO TIP: *Use a towel to put the mixing bowl onto your mixer, as the edges will be very hot from the steam.*

Assembly

After the cupcakes have cooled, use an apple corer to remove the center from each cupcake. Squeeze the Banana Cream Filling inside each cupcake and frost with Mini's Matterhorn Frosting. Sprinkle the top of each cupcake with toasted coconut.

Berry Lemon

Mini's Blueberry Hill Sour Cream and Lemon Cupcakes
Lemon Curd Filling
Lemon Cream Cheese Frosting
Fresh blueberries for decoration

Makes 30 cupcakes in perfectly cute 2-ounce soufflé cups

wet ingredients

　　　Whole blueberries
1/2　cup sour cream
1/2　cup blueberry purée
1/2　cup unsweetened applesauce
1/2　cup soybean oil
　　　Zest of 1 lemon
 2　　eggs
 1　　tablespoon vanilla

dry ingredients

2 1/4　cups unbleached flour
 1　　cup sugar
 2　　tablespoons baking powder
1/2　teaspoon salt

MINI'S BLUEBERRY HILL SOUR CREAM AND LEMON CUPCAKES

BEFORE YOU START: *Preheat oven to 350 degrees F.*

Place 30 soufflé cups on a flat baking sheet lined with parchment paper or a Silpat.

Place an 18-inch pastry bag with tip inside a large cup with the outside edge hanging over. You will use this to fill the soufflé cups with cupcake batter.

1. Drop a couple of whole blueberries into each soufflé cup. Set aside.

2. Place remaining wet ingredients together in a mixing bowl. Mix on low speed with a wire whisk attachment for about 1 minute until all ingredients are blended.

3. Combine all dry ingredients in a separate bowl and stir with a spoon to combine.

4. Add dry ingredients to wet ingredients and blend on low speed for 15 seconds until combined. Batter will be lumpy. Scrape down the bowl and turn mixer on high for 30 seconds. Scrape down bowl again, and return to high for another 30 seconds.

Berry Lemon continued

5. Pour batter into prepared pastry bag, then carefully pick up bag and hold the tip upright to prevent the batter from spilling out. Fill the soufflé cups half full.

6. Bake cupcakes for 24 minutes. They are done when you can apply light pressure to the top of a cupcake and it bounces back.

PRO TIP: *To make $1/2$ cup of an amazing blueberry purée, cook 2 cups berries with a small amount of water until they are soft. Then use an immersion blender to process until smooth. Let the mix cool before using.*

3	lemons
1	cup lemon juice
$1/2$	cup granulated sugar
2	eggs
1	cup unsalted butter, room temperature

LEMON CURD FILLING

Fills 25 to 30 cupcakes

1. Zest the lemons into a double boiler. Juice the lemons into a glass measuring cup and then add enough lemon juice to equal 1 cup. Add lemon juice, sugar, and eggs to the double boiler and whisk until egg mixture is thoroughly mixed with the lemon juice and zest.

2. Cut butter into small pieces and add to mixture; whisk until butter is melted. Continue to whisk occasionally; the mixture will thicken slightly. This takes about 20 minutes.

3. Let the mixture cool in the fridge completely before using. As the lemon curd cools, it will thicken even more. Use squeeze bottles to fill cupcakes and store up to 1 week.

1 (8-ounce) package cream cheese, room temperature
1 teaspoon vanilla
1 lemon
4 cups powdered sugar

LEMON CREAM CHEESE FROSTING

Frosts 25 to 30 cupcakes

1. In a mixing bowl with a wire whisk attachment, beat the cream cheese and vanilla for 3 to 4 minutes. Continually scrape down sides of bowl to ensure all the cream cheese is creamy and well blended. Zest the lemon into the bowl and add the juice from the lemon to the mixture.

2. Add the powdered sugar, $1/2$ cup at a time, to the cream cheese mixture. Mix in each addition of the powdered sugar completely, as this will eliminate lumps. Scrape down the bowl often.

Assembly

After the cupcakes have cooled, use an apple corer to remove the center from each cupcake. Squeeze the Lemon Curd Filling inside each cupcake and frost with Lemon Cream Cheese Frosting; top each cupcake with two or three blueberries.

COFFEE & LIBATIONS

Lemon Drop
77

Mocha Latte
87

Margaritaville
79

Carrie Cosmo
91

Tiramisu
83

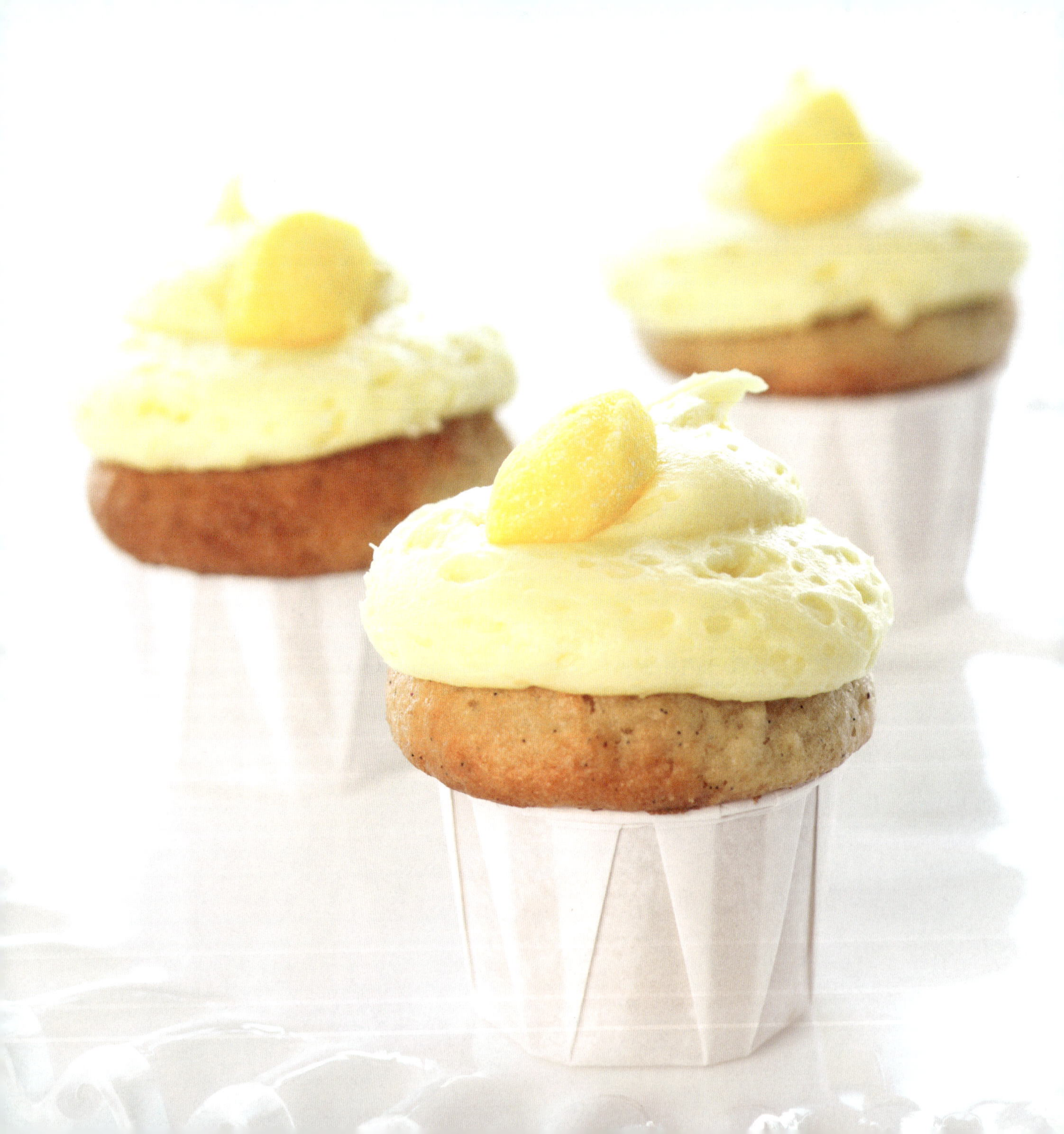

Lemon Drop

Mini's Lemonicious Cupcakes
Citron Vodka
Lemon Cream Cheese Frosting
Lemon drops for decoration

Makes 30 cupcakes in perfectly cute 2-ounce soufflé cups

wet ingredients

Zest of 3 lemons
Juice of 3 lemons, with enough milk added to the lemon juice to equal ¾ cup of liquid
¼ cup sour cream
½ cup unsweetened applesauce
¼ cup soybean oil
¼ cup unsalted butter, room temperature
3 eggs
2 tablespoons vanilla

dry ingredients

2½ cups unbleached flour
1½ cups sugar
2 tablespoons baking powder
½ teaspoon salt

MINI'S LEMONICIOUS CUPCAKES

BEFORE YOU START: *Preheat oven to 350 degrees F.*

Place 30 soufflé cups on a flat baking sheet lined with parchment paper or a Silpat.

Place an 18-inch pastry bag with tip inside a large cup with the outside edge hanging over. You will use this to fill the soufflé cups with cupcake batter.

1. Place all wet ingredients together in a mixing bowl. Mix on low speed with a wire whisk attachment for about 1 minute until all ingredients are blended.

2. Combine all dry ingredients in a separate bowl and stir with a spoon to combine.

3. Add dry ingredients to wet ingredients and blend on low speed for 15 seconds until combined. Batter will be lumpy. Scrape down the bowl and turn mixer on high for 30 seconds. Scrape down the bowl again, and return to high for another 30 seconds.

4. Pour batter into prepared pastry bag, then carefully pick up bag and hold the tip upright to prevent batter from spilling out. Fill the soufflé cups half full.

5. Bake cupcakes for 24 minutes. They are done when you can apply light pressure to the top of a cupcake and it bounces back.

Lemon Drop
continued

- 1 (8-ounce) package cream cheese, room temperature
- 1 teaspoon vanilla
- 1 lemon
- 4 cups powdered sugar

LEMON CREAM CHEESE FROSTING

Frosts 25 to 30 cupcakes

1. In a mixing bowl with a wire whisk attachment, beat the cream cheese and vanilla for 3 to 4 minutes. Continually scrape down sides of bowl to ensure all the cream cheese is creamy and well blended. Zest the lemon into the bowl and add the juice from the lemon to the mixture.

2. Add the powdered sugar, 1/2 cup at a time, to the cream cheese mixture. Mix in each addition of the powdered sugar completely, as this will eliminate lumps. Scrape down the bowl often.

Assembly

After the cupcakes have cooled, dip the top of each one—still in the soufflé cup—in the citron vodka. Frost with Lemon Cream Cheese Frosting and top each cupcake with a lemon drop.

Margaritaville

Key Largo Lime Cupcakes
Tequila
Margarita Cream Cheese Frosting
White sanding sugar for decoration
Lime zest

Makes 30 cupcakes in perfectly cute 2-ounce soufflé cups

wet ingredients

Zest of 5 Key limes
Juice of 5 Key limes, with enough milk added to the lime juice to equal ¾ cup of liquid
¼ cup sour cream
½ cup unsweetened applesauce
½ cup soybean oil
3 eggs
2 tablespoons vanilla

dry ingredients

2½ cups unbleached flour
1½ cups sugar
1 tablespoon baking powder
½ teaspoon salt

KEY LARGO LIME CUPCAKES

BEFORE YOU START: *Preheat oven to 350 degrees F.*

Place 30 soufflé cups on a flat baking sheet lined with parchment paper or a Silpat.

Place an 18-inch pastry bag with tip inside a large cup with the outside edge hanging over. You will use this to fill the soufflé cups with cupcake batter.

1. Place all wet ingredients together in a mixing bowl. Mix on low speed with a wire whisk attachment for about 1 minute until all ingredients are blended.

2. Combine all dry ingredients in a separate bowl and stir with a spoon to combine.

3. Add dry ingredients to wet ingredients and blend on low speed for 15 seconds until combined. Batter will be lumpy. Scrape down the bowl and turn mixer on high for 30 seconds. Scrape down bowl again, and return to high for another 30 seconds.

4. Pour batter into prepared pastry bag, then carefully pick up bag and hold the tip upright to prevent the batter from spilling out. Fill the soufflé cups half full.

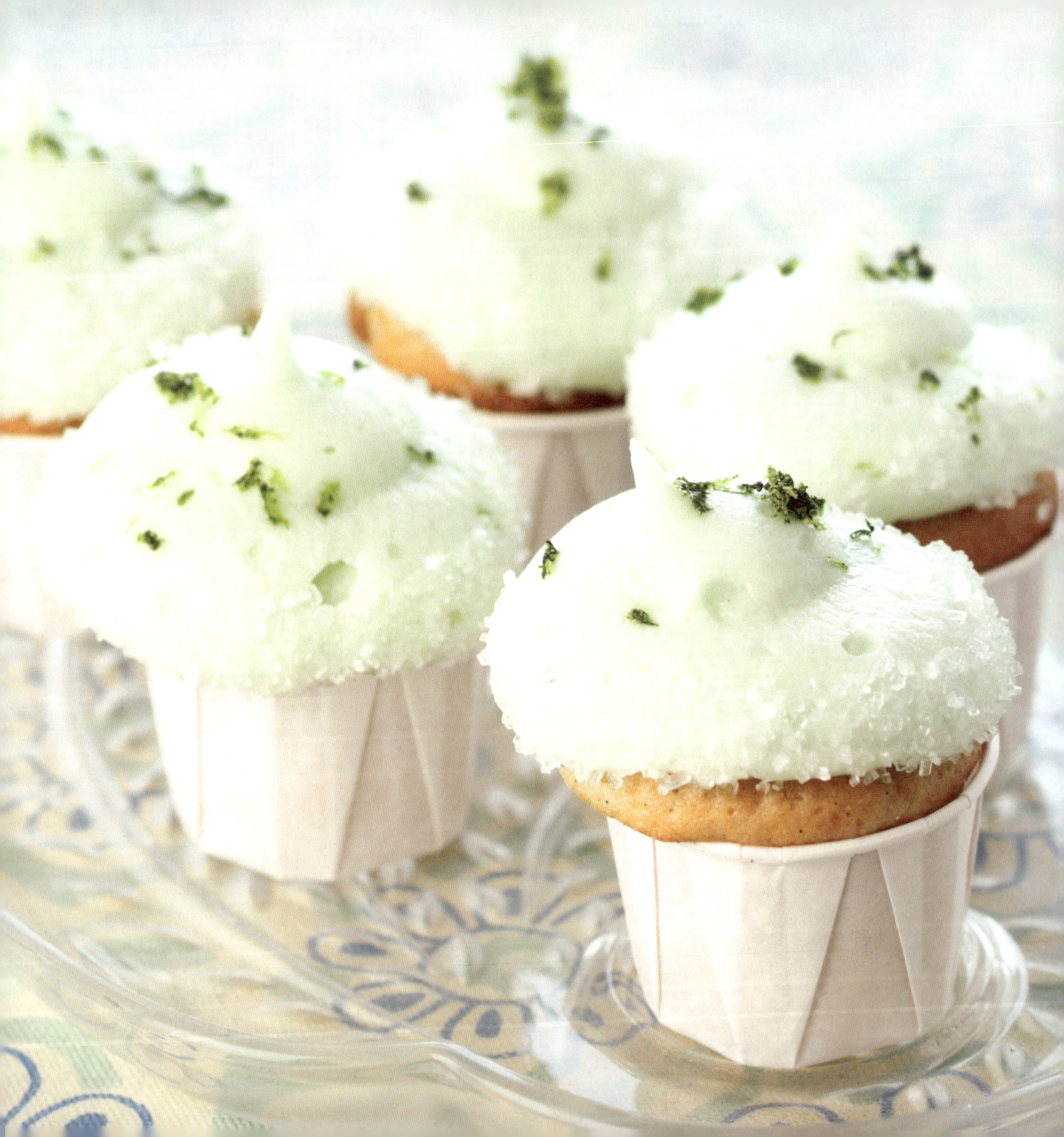

Margaritaville continued

5. Bake cupcakes for 24 minutes. They are done when you can apply light pressure to the top of a cupcake and it bounces back.

PRO TIP: *Use Key limes in this recipe if you can. Key limes are much smaller but more intense in flavor than their cousins, the larger Persian variety.*

- 1 (8-ounce) package cream cheese, room temperature
- 1 teaspoon vanilla
- ¼ cup margarita mix (dry)
- 4 cups powdered sugar

MARGARITA CREAM CHEESE FROSTING

Frosts 25 to 30 cupcakes

1. In a mixing bowl with a wire whisk attachment, beat the cream cheese, vanilla, and margarita mix for 3 to 4 minutes. Continually scrape down sides of bowl to ensure all the cream cheese is creamy and well blended.

2. Add the powdered sugar, ½ cup at a time, to the cream cheese mixture. Mix in each addition of the powdered sugar completely, as this will eliminate lumps. Scrape down the bowl often.

Assembly

After cupcakes have cooled, dip the top of each one—still in the soufflé cup—in the tequila. Frost with Margarita Cream Cheese Frosting. Roll the edges of the frosting in the white sanding sugar to emulate a salt rim, and top each cupcake with a bit of lime zest.

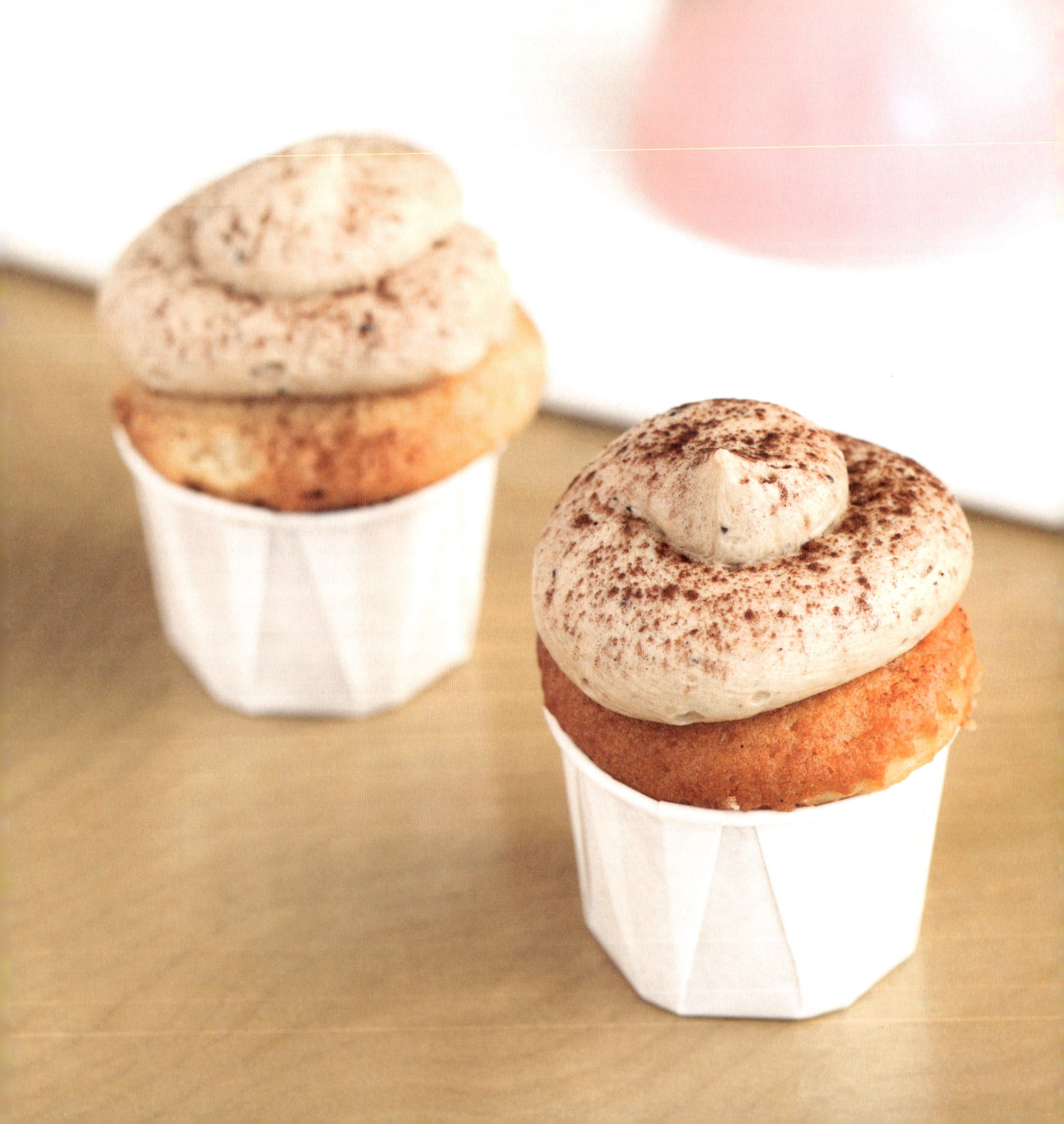

Tiramisu

Mini's Buttery Vanilla Cupcakes
Dark Rum
Espresso
Mocha Latte Frosting
Cocoa powder for decoration

Makes 30 cupcakes in perfectly cute 2-ounce soufflé cups

wet ingredients

- ¼ cup sour cream
- ¼ cup buttermilk
- ½ cup unsweetened applesauce
- ½ cup soybean oil
- ¼ cup unsalted butter, room temperature
- 2 large eggs
- 1 egg yolk
- 2 tablespoons vanilla
- 1 tablespoon vanilla bean paste

dry ingredients

- 2 cups unbleached flour
- 1 cup sugar
- 1¼ tablespoons baking powder
- ½ teaspoon salt

MINI'S BUTTERY VANILLA CUPCAKES

BEFORE YOU START: *Preheat oven to 350 degrees F.*

Place 30 soufflé cups on a flat baking sheet lined with parchment paper or a Silpat.

Place an 18-inch pastry bag with tip inside a large cup with the outside edge hanging over. You will use this to fill the soufflé cups with cupcake batter.

1. Place all wet ingredients together in a mixing bowl. Mix on low speed with a wire whisk attachment for about 1 minute until all ingredients are blended.

2. Combine all dry ingredients in a separate bowl and stir with a spoon to combine.

3. Add dry ingredients to wet ingredients and blend on low for 1 minute until combined. Batter will be lumpy but blended. Scrape down the sides of the bowl. Turn mixer on high for 30 seconds; most of the lumps will disappear and small air bubbles will start to form.

4. Pour batter into prepared pastry bag, then carefully pick up bag and hold the tip upright to prevent the batter from spilling out. Fill the soufflé cups half full.

5. Bake for 17 minutes. Cupcakes are done when you can apply light pressure to the top of the cupcake and it bounces back.

Tiramisu
continued

  5   egg whites, room temperature
1 1/8 cups granulated sugar
       Pinch salt
  1   teaspoon vanilla
  2   cups unsalted butter, room temperature
  1   shot (2 ounces) espresso or very strong coffee
 1/4   cup freshly ground coffee
  2   cups powdered sugar

MOCHA LATTE FROSTING

Frosts 25 to 30 cupcakes

1. In a mixing bowl, whisk egg whites, sugar, and salt. Place the mixing bowl over a pan of simmering water. Whisk the mixture every couple of minutes to ensure the sugar granules along the side of the bowl are fully melted with the egg. Continue to whisk until temperature reaches 174 degrees F.

2. Remove bowl from the pan of simmering water and beat mixture on high using a wire whisk until the bottom of the bowl no longer retains any heat and the mixture reaches a stiff peak consistency. Add vanilla; whisk until incorporated.

3. Remove the wire whisk and use the paddle attachment to finish the frosting. With the mixer set on medium-low, add the butter, 1 tablespoon at a time, waiting until each addition of butter is blended in before adding the next. If the frosting becomes curdled, do not worry; just continue to add the butter and beat the frosting, and it will eventually become creamy and smooth.

4. Once all the butter is incorporated and the mixture is creamy and smooth, add the espresso and ground coffee. Rewhip. Add the powdered sugar, 1/2 cup at a time, until all sugar is added and frosting becomes slightly stiff.

PRO TIP: *For a really strong coffee flavor, make sure you use espresso. Regular brewed coffee will dilute the coffee taste.*

Assembly

After your cupcakes have cooled, dip the top of each one—still in the soufflé cup—in the rum and espresso. Frost with Mocha Latte Frosting. Sprinkle cocoa powder on top of each cupcake for decoration.

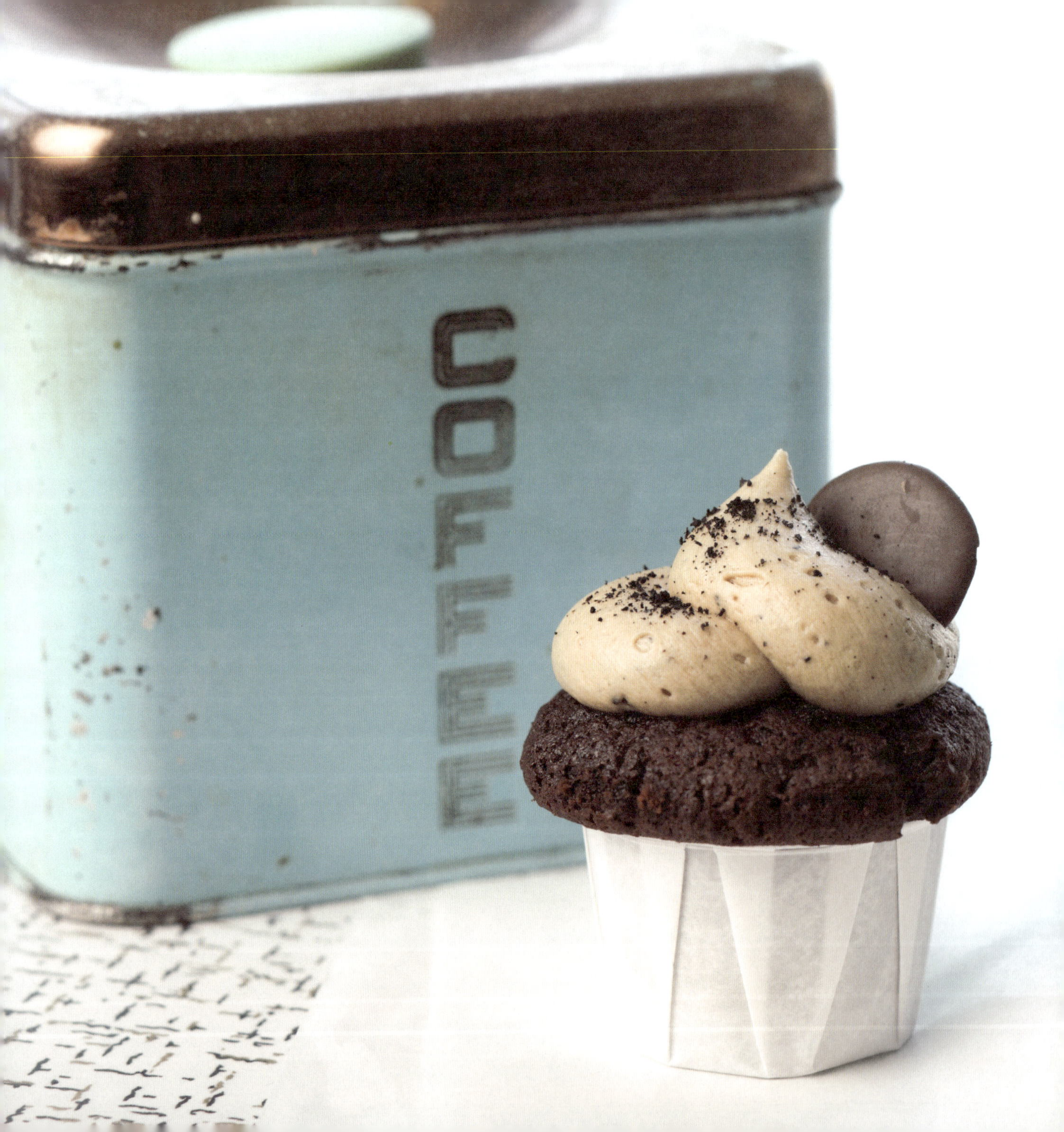
COFFEE

Mocha Latte

Mini's Chocoholic Cupcakes
Mocha Latte Frosting
Freshly ground coffee and chocolate discs for decoration

Makes 30 cupcakes in perfectly cute 2-ounce soufflé cups

chocolate ingredients

- ½ cup Guittard Extra-Dark Chocolate Chips, at least 62 percent cacao
- ½ cup boiling water, strong coffee or espresso

wet ingredients

- ½ cup unsweetened applesauce
- ½ cup soybean oil
- 2 large eggs
- 1 tablespoon vanilla

dry ingredients

- 1½ cups unbleached flour
- 1 cup sugar
- 1 tablespoon baking powder
- ½ teaspoon salt
- ½ cup Dutch-process cocoa powder

MINI'S CHOCOHOLIC CUPCAKES

BEFORE YOU START: *Preheat oven to 350 degrees F.*

Place 30 soufflé cups on a flat baking sheet lined with parchment paper or a Silpat.

Place an 18-inch pastry bag with tip inside a large cup with the outside edge hanging over. You will use this to fill the soufflé cups with cupcake batter.

1. In a large glass measuring cup, combine the chocolate and boiling water. Let the chocolate melt in the hot liquid, then stir to combine and set aside.

2. Place all wet ingredients together in a mixing bowl. Mix on low speed with a wire whisk attachment for about 1 minute until all ingredients are blended. Slowly pour the warm chocolate mixture down the side of the bowl while the mixer is on low. Do not add the hot water and chocolate too quickly or you will cook the eggs.

3. Combine all dry ingredients in a separate bowl and stir with a spoon to combine.

4. Add dry ingredients to wet ingredients and blend on low speed for 30 seconds until combined. Batter will be lumpy. Scrape down the bowl and turn your mixer on high for 30 seconds. Scrape down bowl again, and return to high for another 30 seconds.

Mocha Latte
continued

5. Pour batter into prepared pastry bag, then carefully pick up bag and hold the tip upright to prevent the batter from spilling out. Fill the soufflé cups half full.

6. Bake cupcakes for 19 minutes. They are done when you can apply light pressure to the top of the cupcake and it bounces back. Also watch for a shiny part in the center of the cupcakes; if there is shine, they have not cooked long enough.

PRO TIP: *It is important to use Dutch-process cocoa in this recipe. The normal grocery store variety of cocoa is usually unsweetened but it has not been treated with an alkali to neutralize its natural acidity.*

- 5 egg whites, room temperature
- 1 1/8 cups granulated sugar
- Pinch salt
- 1 teaspoon vanilla
- 2 cups unsalted butter, room temperature
- 1 shot (2 ounces) espresso or very strong coffee
- 1/4 cup freshly ground coffee
- 2 cups powdered sugar

MOCHA LATTE FROSTING

Frosts 25 to 30 cupcakes

1. In a mixing bowl, whisk egg whites, sugar, and salt. Place the mixing bowl over a pan of simmering water. Whisk the mixture every couple of minutes to ensure the sugar granules along the side of the bowl are fully melted with the egg. Continue to whisk until temperature reaches 174 degrees F.

2. Remove bowl from the pan of simmering water and beat mixture on high using a wire whisk until the bottom of the bowl no longer retains any heat and the mixture reaches a stiff peak consistency. Add vanilla; whisk until incorporated.

3. Remove the wire whisk and use the paddle attachment to finish the frosting. With the mixer set on medium-low, add the butter, 1 tablespoon at a time, waiting until each

addition of butter is blended in before adding the next. If the frosting becomes curdled, do not worry; just continue to add the butter and beat the frosting, and it will eventually become creamy and smooth.

4. Once all the butter is incorporated and the frosting is creamy and smooth, add the espresso and ground coffee. Rewhip. Add the powdered sugar, 1/2 cup at a time, until all sugar is added and frosting becomes slightly stiff.

PRO TIP: *For a really strong coffee flavor, make sure you use espresso. Regular brewed coffee will dilute the coffee taste.*

---

1 cup dark chocolate or chocolate bark pieces

DECORATIVE CHOCOLATE DISCS

Makes about 12 discs

1. Melt chocolate in a glass bowl in the microwave or in a metal bowl over a pan of simmering water, stirring frequently. When chocolate is melted and smooth, use a teaspoon and pour a small amount on a chilled flat baking sheet lined with parchment paper. Repeat with remaining melted chocolate. Place in refrigerator and chill. Use discs to decorate the top of cupcakes.

Assembly

After the cupcakes have cooled, frost with Mocha Latte Frosting. Sprinkle the top of each cupcake with freshly ground coffee and a chocolate disc.

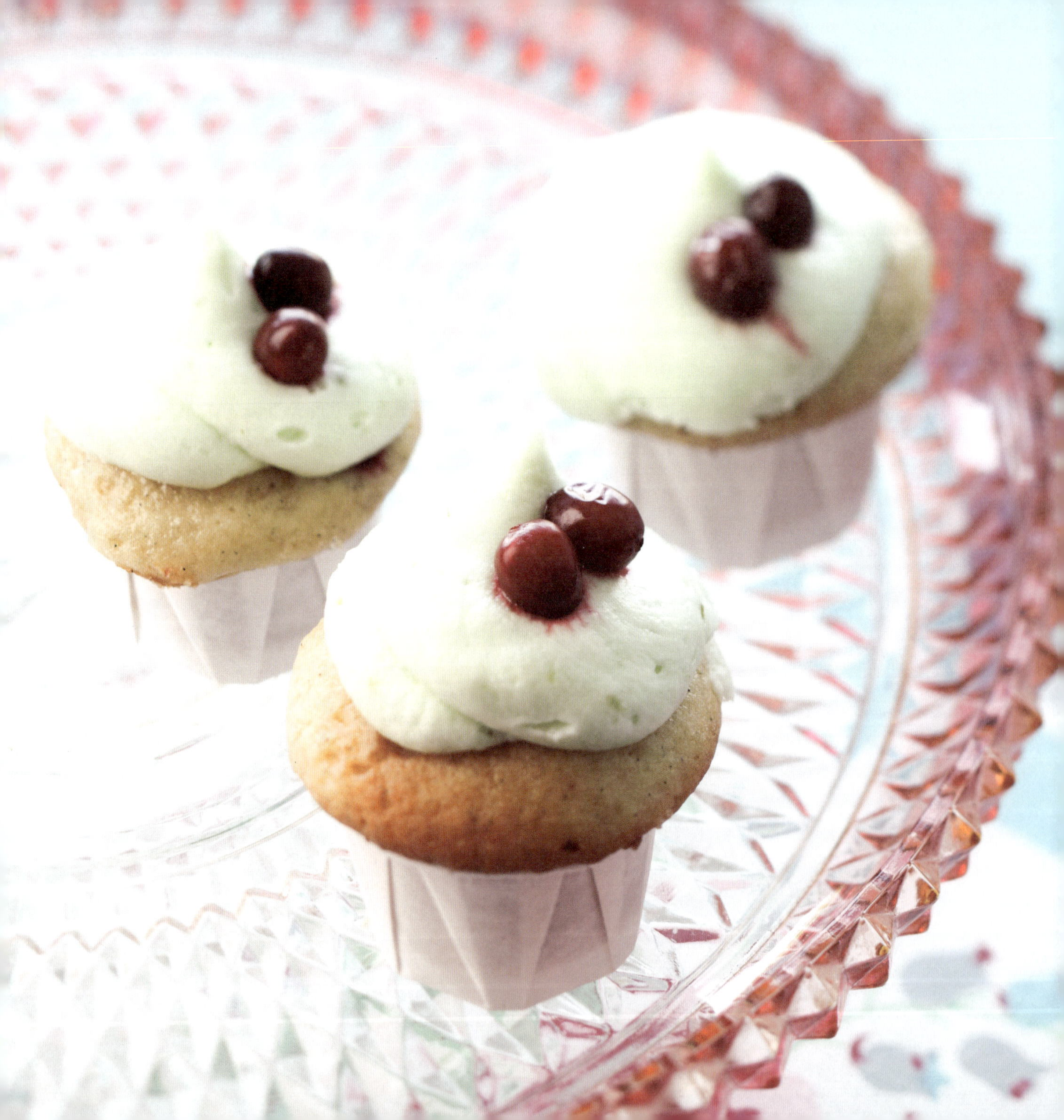

Carrie Cosmo

Mini's Cranberry Vanilla Cupcakes
Cranberry Juice
Vodka
Margarita Cream Cheese Frosting
Fresh or frozen whole cranberries for decoration

Makes 30 cupcakes in perfectly cute 2-ounce soufflé cups

wet ingredients

- Whole cranberries
- ¼ cup sour cream
- ¼ cup buttermilk
- ½ cup unsweetened applesauce
- ½ cup soybean oil
- ¼ cup unsalted butter, room temperature
- 2 large eggs
- 1 egg yolk
- 1 teaspoon vanilla
- ½ cup smashed frozen cranberries

dry ingredients

- 2 cups unbleached flour
- 1 cup sugar
- 1¼ tablespoons baking powder
- ½ teaspoon salt

MINI'S CRANBERRY VANILLA CUPCAKES

BEFORE YOU START: *Preheat oven to 350 degrees F.*

Place 30 soufflé cups on a flat baking sheet lined with parchment paper or a Silpat.

Place an 18-inch pastry bag with tip inside a large cup with the outside edge hanging over. You will use this to fill the soufflé cups with cupcake batter.

1. Drop 3 or 4 whole cranberries inside each soufflé cup. Set aside.

2. Place remaining wet ingredients together in a mixing bowl. Mix on low speed with a wire whisk attachment for about 1 minute until all ingredients are blended.

3. Combine all dry ingredients in a separate bowl and stir with a spoon to combine.

4. Add dry ingredients to wet ingredients and blend on low for 1 minute until combined. Batter will be lumpy but blended. Turn mixer on high for 30 seconds; most of the lumps will disappear and small air bubbles will start to form.

Carrie Cosmo continued

5. Pour batter into prepared pastry bag, then carefully pick up bag and hold the tip upright to prevent the batter from spilling out. Fill the soufflé cups half full.

6. Bake cupcakes for 17 minutes. They are done when you can apply light pressure to the top of a cupcake and it bounces back.

- 1 (8-ounce) package cream cheese, room temperature
- 1 teaspoon vanilla
- ¼ cup margarita mix (dry)
- 4 cups powdered sugar

MARGARITA CREAM CHEESE FROSTING

Frosts 25 to 30 cupcakes

1. In a mixing bowl with a wire whisk attachment, beat the cream cheese, vanilla, and margarita mix for 3 to 4 minutes. Continually scrape down sides of bowl to ensure all the cream cheese is creamy and well blended.

2. Add the powdered sugar, ½ cup at a time, to the cream cheese mixture. Mix in each addition of the powdered sugar completely, as this will eliminate lumps. Scrape down the bowl often.

Assembly

After the cupcakes have cooled, dip the top of each one—still in the soufflé cup—in a mixture of cranberry juice and vodka. Frost each cupcake with Margarita Cream Cheese Frosting and top with 3 or 4 cranberries.

index

Bolded numbers in index entries indicate a photograph.

A
Audrey, The, 11–13, **12**

B
Banana Cream Filling, 69
Berry Lemon, 71–73
Black and White, **26**–29

C
Caramel
    Mini's Sweet and Salty, 43–45
    Salted Caramel Filling, 37
    Twisted Sister, **34**–37
Carrie Cosmo, **90**–92
"CHIP's" The Ponch
    and Jon, **46**–48
Chocoholic, The, **30**–33
Chocolate, 20–57, 82–89
    Black and White, **26**–29
    "CHIP's" The Ponch
        and Jon, **46**–48
    The Chocoholic, **30**–33
    Cookie Monster, 39–42, **40**
    Dark Chocolate Ganache
        Frosting, 15
    Decorative Chocolate Discs, 25
    The Diva, **22**–25
    Mini's Chocoholic
        Cupcakes, 23
    Mini's Sweet and Salty, 43–45
    Mocha Latte, **86**–89
    PB Fix, 49–51, **50**
    S'Mores Please, **52**–55
    Tainted Love, 14–15
    Tiramisu, **82**–85
    Twisted Sister, **34**–37
    White Chocolate Ganache
        Frosting, 41
Coconut
    Mary Ann, 67–70, **68**
    Snowball, **16**–19
Cookie Monster, 39–42, **40**
Coffee
    Mini's Chocoholic
        Cupcakes, 23
    Mocha Latte, **86**–89
    Mocha Latte Frosting, 84
    Tiramisu, **82**–85
Cranberry
    Carrie Cosmo, **90**–92
    Mini's Cranberry Vanilla
        Cupcakes, 91
Cream cheese
    The Audrey, 11–13, **12**
    Berry Lemon, 71–73
    Carrie Cosmo, **90**–92
    The Diva, **22**–25
    Lemon Cream Cheese
        Frosting, 73
    Lemon Drop, **76**–78
    Margaritaville, 79–81, **80**
    Margarita Cream Cheese
        Frosting, 81
    Mini's Cream Cheese
        Frosting, 10
    Pretty in Pink, **8**–10
    Southern Comfort, 56–57
Cupcakes
    Key Largo Lime Cupcakes, 61
    Mini's Blueberry Hill
        Sour Cream and
        Lemon Cupcakes, 71
    Mini's Buttery Vanilla
        Cupcakes, 9
    Mini's Chocoholic
        Cupcakes, 23
    Mini's Cranberry Vanilla
        Cupcakes, 91
    Mini's Lemonicious
        Cupcakes, 64
    Mini's Red Velvet Cupcakes, 56

D
Dark Chocolate Ganache
    Frosting, 15
Decorative Chocolate Discs, 25
Diva, The, **22**–25

F
Fillings
    Banana Cream Filling, 69
    Key Lime Curd Filling, 62

Lemon Curd Filling, 65
Salted Caramel Filling, 37
Frostings
    Dark Chocolate Ganache
        Frosting, 15
    Lemon Cream Cheese
        Frosting, 73
    Margarita Cream Cheese
        Frosting, 81
    Matterhorn Buttercream
        Frosting, 18
    Milk Chocolate Buttercream
        Frosting, 48
    Mini's Cream Cheese
        Frosting, 10
    Mini's Matterhorn Frosting, 54
    Mocha Latte Frosting, 84
    Peanut Butter Frosting, 44
    White Chocolate Ganache
        Frosting, 41
Fruit, 58–73, 76–81, 90–92
    Berry Lemon, 71–73
    Carrie Cosmo, **90**–92
    Key Largo Pie, **60**–63
    Key Largo Lime Cupcakes, 61
    Key Lime Curd Filling, 62
    Lemon Cream Cheese
        Frosting, 73
    Lemon Curd Filling, 65
    Lemon Drop, **76**–78
    Lemon Pie, 64–66

Mary Ann, 67–70, **68**
Mini's Blueberry Hill
    Sour Cream and
    Lemon Cupcakes, 71
Mini's Cranberry Vanilla
    Cupcakes, 91
Mini's Lemonicious
    Cupcakes, 64

G
Graham crackers
    S'Mores Please, **52**–55

K
Key Largo Lime Cupcakes, 61
Key Largo Pie, **60**–63
Key Lime Curd Filling, 62

L
Lemon
    Berry Lemon, 71–73
    Lemon Cream Cheese
        Frosting, 73
    Lemon Curd Filling, 65
    Lemon Drop, **76**–78
    Lemon Pie, 64–66
    Mini's Blueberry Hill
        Sour Cream and
        Lemon Cupcakes, 71
    Mini's Lemonicious
        Cupcakes, 64
Lemon Cream Cheese
    Frosting, 73

Lemon Curd Filling, 65
Lemon Drop, **76**–78
Lemon Pie, 64–66
Lime
    Key Largo Lime Cupcakes, 61
    Key Largo Pie, **60**–63
    Key Lime Curd Filling, 62
    Margaritaville, 79–81, **80**

M
Margarita Cream Cheese
    Frosting, 81
Margaritaville, 79–81, **80**
Mary Ann, 67–70, **68**
Matterhorn Buttercream
    Frosting, 18
Meringue
    Key Largo Pie, **60**–63
    Lemon Pie, 64–66
    Mini's Matterhorn
        Frosting, 54
    S'Mores Please, **52**–55
Milk Chocolate Buttercream
    Frosting, 48
Mini's Blueberry Hill Sour
    Cream and Lemon
    Cupcakes, 71
Mini's Buttery Vanilla
    Cupcakes, 9
Mini's Chocoholic Cupcakes, 23
Mini's Cranberry Vanilla
    Cupcakes, 91

Mini's Cream Cheese
    Frosting, 10
Mini's Lemonicious
    Cupcakes, 64
Mini's Matterhorn Frosting, 54
Mini's Red Velvet Cupcakes, 56
Mini's Sweet and Salty, 43–45
Mocha Latte, **86**–89
Mocha Latte Frosting, 84

P
PB Fix, 49–51, **50**
Peanut Butter Frosting, 44
Peanuts
    Mini's Sweet and
        Salty, 43–45
    PB Fix, 49–51, **50**
Pecans
    Southern Comfort, 56–57
Pretty in Pink, **8**–10
Pretzels
    Twisted Sister, **34**–37

R
Red Velvet Cupcakes, Mini's, 56
Rum
    Tiramisu, **82**–85

S
Salted Caramel Filling, 37
S'Mores Please, **52**–55
Snowball, **16**–19
Southern Comfort, 56–57

T
Tainted Love, 14–15
Tequila
    Margaritaville, 79–81, **80**
Tiramisu, **82**–85
Twisted Sister, **34**–37

V
Vanilla, 6–19, 43, 46, 67, 82, 90
    The Audrey, 11–13, **12**
    Carrie Cosmo, **90**–92
    "CHIP's" The Ponch
        and Jon, **46**–48
    Mary Ann, 67–70, **68**
    Matterhorn Buttercream
        Frosting, 18

Mini's Buttery Vanilla
    Cupcakes, 9
Mini's Cranberry Vanilla
    Cupcakes, 91
Mini's Sweet and Salty, 43–45
Pretty in Pink, **8**–10
Snowball, **16**–19
Tainted Love, 14–15
Tiramisu, **82**–85
Vodka
    Carrie Cosmo, **90**–92
    Lemon Drop, **76**–78

W
White Chocolate Ganache
    Frosting, 41

Metric Conversion Chart

Volume Measurements		Weight Measurements		Temperature Conversion	
U.S.	Metric	U.S.	Metric	Fahrenheit	Celsius
1 teaspoon	5 ml	½ ounce	15 g	250	120
1 tablespoon	15 ml	1 ounce	30 g	300	150
¼ cup	60 ml	3 ounces	90 g	325	160
⅓ cup	75 ml	4 ounces	115 g	350	180
½ cup	125 ml	8 ounces	225 g	375	190
⅔ cup	150 ml	12 ounces	350 g	400	200
¾ cup	175 ml	1 pound	450 g	425	220
1 cup	250 ml	2¼ pounds	1 kg	450	230

ACKNOWLEDGMENTS

After testing and retesting my recipes in my test kitchen (thanks to Karin and her neighborhood crew), I have come to realize that bakers come in many degrees of baking skill level. As an experienced baker, I have learned a great deal from the novice to semipro, who have helped me through this process. I have learned how to adapt my large-quantity baking in a commercial kitchen to small batches that are made at home, with children playing underfoot and in the sink, the doorbell and phone constantly ringing, and all the while socializing with good friends. I must say this process has reminded me why I love to bake all over again.

I would like to say a special thank-you to those that have been particularly helpful through this process. First to my loving and tolerant husband Clair. He has encouraged me to be ME, whatever that ME is from one year to the next—thank you very much for all your support and comfort you provide to me when I have had a particularly bad day.

Second, Karin, what can I say? You have opened up your home, your life, your entire neighborhood (mostly Court), and most of all your heart to me as a friend. All women should be as lucky as I am to have someone like you in their lives.

And lastly, to my staff at Mini's: you have all been a huge support and I am lucky to have a staff willing to put up with my antics, my diva moments, my stress, and my absence during the writing of this cookbook.